SOME REVIEWS OF GARRY KILWORTH'S BOOKS

His characters are strong and the sense of place he creates is immediate. (*Sunday Times* on *In Solitary*)

The Songbirds Of Pain is excellently crafted. Kilworth is a master of his trade. (*Punch Magazine*)

Garry Kilworth is arguably the finest writer of short fiction today, in any genre. (*New Scientist*)

A subtle, poetic novel about the power of place - in this case the South Arabian Deserts - and the lure of myth. It haunted me long after it ended. (*City Limits Magazine* on *Spiral Winds*)

Full of hope, irony and despair and as moving in its understated way as *Riddley Walker*, the last post-apocalypse novel worth paying hard cash for. (*Time Out Magazine* on *Abandonati*)

Atmospherically overcharged like an impending thunderstorm. (*The Guardian* on *Witchwater Country*)

An utterly original and important work that promotes is author to the first rank. (*Newsagent and Bookshop* on *The Night Of Kadar*)

A convincing display of fine talent. (*The Times* on *A Theatre Of Timesmiths*)

Kilworth is one of the most significant writers in the English language. (*Fear Magazine* on *Cloudrock*)

A rich and beautiful novel, uplifting, exciting . . . intelligent, quick and humorous, the positive praises flow forth unhindered when reading this splendid story. (*Swedish Library Service* on *Hunter's Moon*)

A masterpiece of balanced and enigmatic storytelling . . . Kilworth has mastered the form. (*Times Literary Supplement* on *In The Country Of Tattooed Men*)

Children who enjoy rich, evocative language will be well served here: some of Kilworth's (tales), as in the 'The Goblin Jag', are magnificent. (*Times Educational Supplement* on *Dark Hills, Hollow Clocks*)

An absolute delight, based on the myths and legends of the Polynesian peoples. (Mark Morris on *The Roof Of Voyaging*, *SFX Magazine*)

Rich and detailed legends are woven with myth and fiction in this great fantasy. The final volume of a wonderful trilogy. (Aaron Baker on *Land Of Mists, Black Tears*)

A beautiful ending to an excellent saga. (Sharon Gosling on *Land Of Mists*, *SFX Magazine*)

The characters are fascinating and the author weaves a fantastic and colourful image of life in the animal side of Welkin. (Sarah Hutchinson aged 12, on *Gaslight Geezers*, *Young Adult Review News*)

One is left in no doubt about the high quality of the writing or of Kilworth's talent . . . (*Times Educational Supplement* on *Dark Hills, Hollow Clocks*)

Kilworth's versatile skill at navigating between genres, his outre imagination, his deft and evocative handling of the exotic, his keen insights into human behaviour, his affecting ability to inhabit and communicate an impressive breadth of perspectives across cultural and genre spectrums, and, finally but certainly not least, his deliciously elegant prose, all combine to present a selection of stories whose diversity, originality and poignancy leave me breathless with awe. 'Moby Jack and Other Tall Tales' stands as my favourite book of 2006. (Claude Lalumiere on *Moby Jack And Other Tall Tales*, *Locus Magazine Online*)

Garry Kilworth is probably one of the finest writers of short stories Britain has ever produced. (*Bookstove Online*)

ROOKIE BIKER
IN THE OUTBACK

An Australian Motorcycle Challenge

GARRY KILWORTH

ISBN: 1499364067

ISBN-13: 978-1499364064

My thanks to Ewan Grenenger and Murray Nettheim for their notes on the ride. Also to Ross Buxton and Geoff Vautier, cousins, who kindly loaned me their prepared presentation. And finally thanks to John Hales who dragged me along to training on dirt bikes with him over several counties.

This book is for Dan, Kylie, Lang, Andy, Mick and Richard, the team who got us from B to C.
And of course, not forgetting my mentor Pete Worth, without whom I would never have been daft enough to take part. Pete is also responsible for the cover photo.

The Riders

Vaughan Adams   Lee Bolding   Brian Bosch   Ross Buxton
Frank Cogan   Bill Cooney   Tony Davis   David Davidson
Debra Drummond   Peter Drummond   Andrew Ebert   Bill Edgar
Dave Engstrom   Bill Fee   David Folpp   Ewan Grenengar
John Hales   Peter Hickie   Doug Hogg   Louisa Jade
Garry Kilworth   Neville Lewis   Jim Lightfoot   Warren Limpus
Geoff Madder   Bob Mathieson   Cameron McCarthy   Scott McMullen
Chris Mercer   Graham Meyers   Klaus Misins   Gary Moss
Murray Nettheim   George Pender   Vanessa Priest   Anna Renolds
Frank Smith   Bill Stevenson   Dave Thompson   Andrew Thompson
Michael Tulk   Geoff Vautier   Jack Walker   Josie Watts
Jenny Whitlock   Peter Williamson   Geoff Wilson
Alan Worsfeld   Peter Worth   Roger Zwierlain

To view photographs of the ride go to the following link:-
https://plus.google.com/photos/107661375128193856538/albums/5
252439160781929169

PART ONE

1. BEGINNINGS

You know you're getting on a bit when you're told that the next dog you get will probably outlive you. 'We'd be better to get one from the rescue centre,' said my wife Annette, 'they're often older dogs.' It was reflecting on this very stark and sobering news that made me think, 'I need a challenge. Something that will test me before my bones grow brittle and my mind wanders off to the far side of the moon.'

Have you seen the film 'The World's Fastest Indian' starring Anthony Hopkins? It's a true story about a New Zealander with a passion for motorbikes, who takes his Indian motorcycle to the Salt Lakes in America at the age of 60-something in order to break the world speed record. Well I'm also 60-odd and the movie impressed me. I thought, 'I've got to do something like that before I keel over.' The Australian Postie Bike Challenge is not as magnificent as a world speed attempt, but it did look more my mark. Since I was in Melbourne at the time, it also seemed more appropriate.

It's true about the flies in Australia, they cluster around you like . . . well, like flies. They're not particularly large, like the British cattle-bothering clegs, but they are very, very persistent. They hop around your face like fleas and crawl into all your orifices - up your nose, in the corners of your eyes, in your ears - seeking moisture, and boy are they determined to get it. When I spent six months in Melbourne in 2007 I carried switches broken from a garden hedges and got carpal tunnel from constantly flicking it across my face to clear the ground.

'You should see the flies up in Queensland,' Peter, my Ozzie host told me. 'Big as bloody hippos.'

He was exaggerating of course It's an Ozzie prerogative. But Pete went on to talking about an expedition they do in that state every year, a thing he called the 'Postie Bike Challenge'. 'I'm going to do it one year,' he told me, 'before the bones seize up.'

I met Pete in 1971 on a camp site outside Athens. He was newly married to Carolyn and I was driving home to UK from a 3-year RAF posting in Cyprus. Besides Annette and myself, I had two kids in the VW Beetle, the camping gear, and everything else I owned in the world. Pete and I played table tennis in a Corfu barn where the rain came down in torrents. We kept in touch and visited from time to time.

Peter has done some wild things in his time. He's a competent yachtsman, holds a pilot's licence and has had some adventures in the Australian way that would satisfy Odysseus. His back yard is made for adventures and hearing him talk made me wish I'd emigrated to that land when I was younger. I almost went as an older man. My daughter's family lived there for a few years and Annette and I would have joined them if they'd stayed. Now that Pete has more time on his hands he seeks more adventures and I watch him closely to try to hang on to his coat tails when he finds a good one. I'm not a sailor, but am up for almost anything else. Pete is younger than me by about five years, but we're both in our sixties. Both fairly fit and healthy, me mostly from walking and dashing about a tennis court, but who knows when ill-health will strike a nasty blow, or the years become too heavy.

'That sounds like good fun,' I said. 'Tell me about it.'

I thought he was going to extol the virtues of bicycles. A nice gentle pedal through the rainforests of Northern Queensland. He wasn't. Australian postie bikes are not of the push variety. They are full-blooded pedigree motorcycles. Not big ones, admittedly. 110cc Hondas. But they're still quite fast. I'd seen the local postman zipping about the streets of Melbourne on these machines and presumably they used them in the more remote areas of the land down-under too.

Every year an organisation called Gridley Enterprises buys a batch of old postie bikes from the post office. Gridley is not a charitable organisation in itself but it facilitates donations to Rotary. A participant in the 'challenge' buys his second-hand Honda, flogs it over tarmac, dust road and gravel track, then gives it to Rotary at the end of the rally to dispose of as they will, either passing the bike on to a needy country or selling it and doing the something worthy with the cash. Dan Gridley and Kylie Kidby plot a course, put it on the internet, and wait for would-be riders to contact them. I make light of the organisation it must take: the hard work and logistics must be a nightmare. Apparently they've never lost a rider in the wilderness, though they've had one or two fall by the wayside through injury or illness.

Pete said, 'We should do the ride together. The next one is from Brisbane to Cairns - B to C if you like. It's around 4000 kms, some of it through the Outback, some of it through rainforest.'

We were drinking beers on the veranda of his house on the outskirts of Melbourne, contemplating the antics of a dozen noisy rainbow lorakeets in the branches of a massive tree above our heads.

'I haven't got a licence,' I said at last

Pete blinked. 'What?'

'I haven't got a motorbike licence.'

The grizzled grey beard on his chin twitched.

'Why?'

'Why?' I began to get annoyed, more with my inadequacy than Pete's incredulity. 'Because I never took the test. I rode a bike, once, for a couple of weeks - a 250 Ariel Arrow - but I never got around to passing the test. That was, oh, several hundred years ago, when-I-were-a-lad.'

'Well bloody-well get one then.'

'OK.'

And that was that.

Actually, we were in March at the time. The Postie Bike Challenge took place around September/October. I wasn't going home to UK for a while, so I knew 2007 was out. I'd never get my test and organise another trip out to Oz in three months, not to mention the cost of the enterprise, which was over $4000, excluding air fares and other expenses. It would have to be 2008. Pete however was impatient. He put in for the 2007 run, did it, and then wrote to me in UK and said he would also do the 2008 run, with me and a guy I hadn't yet met, another Pommie friend of Pete's who lived in Leicestershire. John.

As soon as I got home I rang an establishment called the Ipswich Rider School. A pleasant young woman called Sue answered the phone. 'You come along here, darlin',' she said. 'We'll soon have you riding around the Suffolk countryside.' I went along there, and met Claire, Andy, Rob, and my instructor to be, the ever-patient Charlie. Naturally they were all a bit puzzled as to why an ancient old scribe like me suddenly wanted to belt along the A14 on a 650cc Kawasaki Ninja. (I wasn't exactly a born-again biker: this being my initial birth.) I explained it was all a bit tamer than that. I needed to get a licence for a 125cc bike in order to tootle along the Bruce Highway in far-off Oz.

They were all very polite. Not one of them sniggered and they all patted me on the head and said they would do their very best to turn the raw material, this 5 feet 7 inches of effete writer, into a trail-blazing John Surtees - or they might have done, if they weren't half my age and had actually heard of John Surtees. I could see they weren't optimistic.

I wondered who would take on the task of moulding this lump of clay into a mean-machine rider. Claire, dark-haired and attractive, with a lovely smile, also took out riders, but I guessed most of her students were women who wanted to be taught by another female. Andy was tall, lean and rangy, a bit like Clint Eastwood. He had tough-looking features that belied the guy underneath. Andy was actually, like Rob and Charlie, a serious biker who strove to get the best out of young lads who were desperate to get out on the road on two wheels. Rob was shorter, but more solid and tightly packed. He looked like a martial arts instructor. Charlie was something between the two. Like me he wore glasses and had been a military man at one time. It was Charlie who took me on.

Good old patient Charlie.

'I'll get you up to speed,' said Charlie. 'You buy yourself a helmet, jacket and boots, and a develop a good positive attitude.'

First, before I could even plant my bottom on a bike that touched the Queen's highways, I would have to pass the government Compulsory Basic Training test. I felt I was back in the R.A.F. again with TLAs (Three-Letter Abbreviations). Charlie and some others took us in a truck to the site of a disused sugar factory on the edge of Ipswich. I had three fellow students, all very much closer to kindergarten than me. We were each given a motor scooter. There followed an eyesight test (I just squeezed through by squinting in a semblance of Jack Palance playing Ghengis Khan) and a talk on safety. Then we went outside and received instructions on the bikes' controls.

Finally we got to sit on one and tootle around some spaced-out traffic cones, getting the feel of the machine, learning some choreographed handling skills and feeling like Steve McQueen in 'The Great Escape'. After which we had a 'long but important talk' - I forget what it was about, but amongst it was probably a warning about the dangers of forming our own biker gang and challenging the local chapter of Hells Angels. (Adversity had brought us all quite close). Later on in the day we at last burned up the highways and byways of Suffolk for two hours, which I found exhilarating and heady, even though we probably didn't go above 25mph. At the end of the day, having all passed, we relaxed with tea, while the youngest of our group shot away.

'Where are you off to in such a hurry?' asked Charlie.

The youth grinned. I'm 17 today - I'm off to pick up my the new Suzuki bike my mum and dad have bought me.'

He could ride it on the roads now his CBT was under his belt, so long as he wore his L-plates.

For me it was the beginning of on-road lessons, with Charlie riding patiently behind me, the voice over his radio mike gently steering me clear of killing either myself or any unwary pedestrians. I had one nasty moment when I failed to see a car coming (my view was blocked by a parked van) when doing a U-turn. Charlie stepped out into the road and held up his hand traffic-cop-like, to halt the vehicle speeding towards me. I then got a strong lecture on lack of observation.

'Don't follow orders like an automaton,' he chastised me, 'you're riding for yourself, not for me.'

I was to hear that phrase many times, even from the examiner on taking my test - *Ride for yourself.* You were supposed to forget someone was tracking your every move from a few yards behind you. You were supposed to be riding oblivious of that fact. However, when someone's murmuring instructions constantly in your left ear, it's very difficult to imagine you're on your sweet lonesome. It's easy to relinquish responsibility for yourself. Fatal, but very, very easy.

I found the hardest things to do on the bike were the little manoeuvres like U-turns. The bike wasn't as sensitive to the touch as I'd have liked and it wasn't difficult to under or oversteer when trying to U-turn on a narrow council estate road. Touch either curb and you failed. Put your foot down during the exercise, and you failed. Whistle 'Dixie' and you failed. It was very easy to fail the U-turn.

The thing to do was 'look long'. It was deadly to stare at the opposite curb as you turned - because that's where you'd steer the bike. You have to sit up straight and whip your head round halfway through, stare over your shoulder down the long road where you eventually want to be heading. Right up to the test I was never sure I was going to get round without a foot going down. On my first test try I did a perfect U-turn - I failed on something else.

Before I could take the practical test of course, I had to do the theory tests. It's fifty-seven years since I took my first driving test in a 20-year-old Austin 7. That little Austin was a 747cc 'Box Saloon' motorcar which weighed less than its four passengers. Based on the Ford Model T it had all the appearance of an 18th Century black carriage that had lost its horse. A flimsy little vehicle - you could poke your finger through the upholstery - everything connected by wires. Sometimes one of the wires snapped and you would lose the brakes, acceleration or steering: usually something fairly important to a long life.

In those days there was no such thing as theory tests and if there had been, it wouldn't have been taken on a computer. The first part of the exam was the Hazard Test, where I had to play a game as the driver of a car indicating road hazards where they seemed likely to develop. I've never been good with uncontrollable movements on screens and by the fifth hazard I felt desperately motion sick. I did make it through to the fourteenth hazard, then belted for the toilet bowl. When I came out, wiping my mouth, the examiner said wryly, 'Mr Kilworth, the good news is, you don't have to take it again.' I'd passed. And I also passed the multi-choice questions. I'd taken that as a given anyway: I've always been good with ticks and crosses on paper. It was the practical exam that I was concerned with, and I was right to be so.

Charlie took me over all the routes the examiner was likely to take me, pointing out the awkward places where I might meet a bus coming towards me, or junctions with strange angles. In the main these did not bother me, nor the emergency stop or anything except the blasted U-turn of course. What did bother me was the fact that I could be on a 40 MPH road without knowing it and could be failed for 'not progressing' or in layman's language, going too slow. Since I was new to the area and was being guided by a bodiless voice all the time I never quite knew where I was most of the time. And some nice local kids had stolen a lot of the 40 MPH repeater signs: those little reminders normally fixed to lamp posts. I often found myself doing 30 MPH on a 40 MPH road.

Andy provided a good solution to this problem.

'If you think you're on a faster road,' he said, 'look down the sideroads. If you see a thirty sign, you know the road you're on must be forty. You might pick up a minor for not progressing for a short distance, but if you do the whole length of the road without speeding up, it'll be a major fault and he's bound to fail you.'

I took my first test in May 2008. I thought I'd done all right.

'I'm afraid on this occasion you haven't passed,' said the examiner. 'Lack of observation.'

'What?' I asked. 'How? Where?'

'On one stretch of the road there were vehicles parked down both sides and a bus coming down the middle.'

'I saw that,' I replied. 'I observed that, all right. I slowed down and changed direction to avoid the bus.'

'True, but you didn't look in your mirror first.'

'I did.'

'Didn't.'

'Did . . .' but of course, I wasn't going to win a playground battle of dids and didn'ts with an omnipotent examiner. I had failed. I felt devastated. He asked me when I wanted to retest and I told him, 'Never.' Of course when I'd cooled down, Charlie and Andy persuaded me to take the thing again, which I did at the end of June. Meanwhile from the far side of the planet Earth Pete was sending gently-encouraging emails like, 'Pass your test you pommy girl's blouse! What's the matter with you? You've got two arms and two legs like everyone else. Don't think with your arse, think with your head. You have got a brain *somewhere* in there, I suppose . . .' and other such helpful rosy phrases.

I did take the test again, of course. I was still totally obsessed with the U-turn, but again it went like a dream. About halfway through the test disaster struck. The examiner had managed to get himself a hundred yards or so behind me, back in traffic. This is not unusual. It's always difficult for someone following behind to keep in touch with the man ahead. I came to a roundabout and, since Charlie had always taken me a certain way, I turned *right*. Even as I began my majestic sweep around the roundabout, having done my *lifesaver* - a brief glance over the right shoulder - I heard a voice in my ear saying, 'Turn left at the roundabout. Take the left turn.' But I was already committed to turning right, and instead of continuing right round the bloody circuit, I panicked and took my usual exit. It was a fast road. I went quarter-of-a-mile before I was able to turn round and begin searching for my lost examiner. The first person I saw was Charlie, who had been following both of us.

'Where is he?' I yelled, panic-stricken. 'Do you know?'

'Somewhere on that housing estate,' replied Charlie in a cool voice. 'Come on, we'll find him . . .'

I followed faithful Charlie, who then left me parked by a curb while he did a square search of the region. He found the examiner and brought him to me. The first thing I asked the examiner, as he removed his helmet, was naturally, 'Have I failed?'

His face was deadpan. He replied quietly and calmly, 'Unfortunately I can't fail you for not following my instructions - only for making an error on the road.' There was a moment's silence while I digested this wonderful, unexpected piece of news, then he added, 'But you'd better be very good after this, Garry,' we were on first name terms now, 'because you've just cost me most of my lunch hour.'

I did pass that day, by the skin of my teeth, and went home to find a short cheerful message on my phone from downunder Pete. 'Well done, Garry' he said, 'congratulations on passing your motorcycle test.' I thought, how the hell does he know? He was in Oz. But of course Pete didn't know. He was guessing. I like to think he had a little faith in this Pom. I was like a two-year-old, full of jumping joy. I was going to Oz to take part in the Postie Bike Challenge! I had passed my bike test and was on my way. It's true to say I was as happy as Larry, which on reflection seems appropriate, since the expression is an Australian one and refers to Australian scallywags, which the Aussies call 'larrikins'. A larrikin is worse than a bloke, but not as bad as a hoon. Hoons drive too fast and drive dangerously, I didn't want to be one of them. No-sir. I just wanted to ride my bike and I wanted to ride it where I liked.

Pete said on the phone, 'Once we start the ride though, you're on your own!'

'Fine,' I replied, 'but don't expect me to share my jolly jumbuck with you when you run out of bread-and-jam.'

2. PLOUGHED FIELDS AND BRIDLEWAYS

With the test now under my belt I had to think about getting some off-road experience on two wheels. Pete insisted on it: there were copious emails from com.au demanding action. John, the other Pom joining Pete and I in Australia, proved to be a brilliant ferret. Or perhaps it was his wife Stephanie? Anyway either John or Steph found and arranged a one-day motocross course near Ipswich for the both of us, to be followed by a trailbike course at St Albans. The motocross course was run by a great guy named Geoff Mayes, who turned out to be one of those people gifted with passing on the secret skills of their science. He was wise in the way of dirt bikes, had the patience of a god, and I am sure could choreograph machines so long as they had two wheels.

John and I met in the car park for the first time. At just over 60-years John was a bit younger than me. We were both grey panthers (a much more acceptable euphemism than *old farts*). At our time of life who you are and what you've achieved is irrelevant. Status is totally unimportant. Age is a great leveller. It doesn't matter whether you've been a company director or a toilet attendant in your working life, if you end up pompous and high-handed, unable to get on with your fellow men, then you're going to have a lonely last-quarter of your life.

Happily for me John was cheerful, open, bright and easy to like. I hope I came across the same way. We were going to spend several weeks in each other's company and it was important that we did not take an instant dislike to each other.

'Want a salmon sandwich?' he asked. 'I've got more in the boot of the car.'

'Thanks,' I replied, 'I will.'

After the sandwich we looked at the blackening sky thoughtfully, then went to meet Geoff Mayes, a greying British motocross champion and an all-round expert on going fast on a dirt bike. Geoff was remarkably ordinary-looking for such a tough competitor, but then I had never met a champion dirt bike rider before. I quickly found that men associated with this daredevil sport, along with their fellows the trailbikers, were generally a smiling affable bunch of guys who just love what they do. They have no need to show off or be anything but themselves. They are the real stuff when it comes to a dangerous and difficult sport.

Geoff greeted us warmly and kitted us out with plastic greaves, chest and back protectors, elbow guards, gloves, motocross helmets, thick boots, goggles, jackets and jeans. I could hardly walk, let alone ride a motorcycle. I felt like one of those knights who had to be winched into the saddle. Ask me to tie my shoelace and I would have burst into tears.

'All right?' asked John, slapping me on the shoulder. 'I'm leaving my glasses off.'

'So am I,' I said.

The motocross goggles tended to crush glasses against one's eyes and a blurred vision was better than having to worry about adjusting things on one's face every five minutes. It was important that we kept our hands free for steering, breaking and accelerating. We only had to look a few yards ahead in any case.

I stared at the track. It was this stony dirt strip that went round and up and down like a switchback for about a kilometre, with hairpin-tight curves and corners, and lonely drops into hidden gorges. I could see one steep hill that was almost a vertical wall. I watched 16 and 18-year-olds hammering round this track on their bikes, taking the hills with flying leaps on their growling machines. My stomach flip-flopped. Only two weeks before today I had been riding a 125cc scooter with L-plates on it. Now I was expected to imitate Evel Knievel. *Can I really do this?* I thought. At that moment it started to rain and the track turned to sludge.

John slapped me on the back again. 'Here we go,' he said, and nudged me towards my 250cc Kawasaki motocross bike, which being off-road I was allowed to play with. One of Geoff Mayes' assistants went with me. He was a thick-set, solid older man who appeared to be fashioned from leather. Fred was as gentle as he was tough-looking, but he was standing no nonsense from this effete writer. 'You'll do a few turns round that little track over there,' he said, 'then on the top section of the big track, then finally on the whole track.'

Will I? I thought. Will I really? I climbed into the saddle of the bike only to find my short legs could not touch the ground. Motocross bikes are extremely tall machines, due I guess to the springs, whatever. My next problem was starting the damn thing. The kick start handle was halfway up the side of the bike and I could not get my leg high enough to work it. Fred gave me a helping foot and the bike coughed into action.

Geoff had given us a little lecture before we started.

'Don't lean over with the bike on going round a corner, like you would on a road bike. Push it away from you, keep your body upright. Sit as far up as near the handlebars as possible - maintain your weight over the front wheel. When you take a hill, give it the gas going up, but ease off the throttle on going over the top or you'll find a lot of air between the ground and the back wheel. Open up the throttle on the straight, but throttle-back on entering a corner. Halfway round the bend open the throttle again. Left-hand bends, stick out the left leg. Right-hand bends, stick out the right leg. Now, off you go!'

John and I went round the small flat track rather timidly at first, then got braver by the minute. Soon we were both bored with playing on the roundabout and went onto the top half of the big track. The mud was slippery but we managed to stay on for several circuits. Then we got bored with that and it was time for the big track. John went hurtling off, spraying mud and grit into air. I followed a bit more cautiously. Those first three times round the big track I almost came off on several corners. God was gracious and somehow I managed to stay in the saddle. But I found it exhausting, mentally, probably because I was physically tense.

I halted after three circuits.

'I'll stop now,' I told Fred, cheerfully, thinking I might as well quit while I was ahead. 'I've got the hang of it. I've had enough practice.'

'Oh no you haven't,' Fred replied, quietly.

'Yes, yes, I have,' I insisted. 'I don't need any more.'

'Oh yes you do,' said Fred, firmly.

The rain was belting down. I was unhappy. I had mud in every orifice. My arms and legs ached. My head hammered.

'Off you go, then,' Fred said. 'Get a few more under your belt - about twenty or so circuits, eh?'

Miserably, I did as I was told - and of course after a few more circuits began to enjoy it. I can do this, I thought. I *can* do this. I wasn't burning up the track like an eighteen-year-old, but I was taking every tight corner at a reasonable speed and getting the hang of handling a bike that like a frisky colt wanted to dance in the slippery mud on its own. It was trying to throw me off, but I stuck to the saddle with determination, roaring up the hills, leaping over the tops, and charging down the gradients. Man and machine did not exactly become one, but we certainly came to respect one another as individuals. At the end of the day I felt charged, exhilarated and a little more macho.

This feeling was soon knocked out of me when John and I went on another course, this time at St Albans. We booked in for a day with Trailworld who take potential dirt bikers out on a tour of the muddy lanes and green roads, such as the Icknield Way, even across ploughed fields. Again the bikes were taller than fully-grown race horses. High, heavy beasts that I had great difficulty in getting my short leg over, let alone doing anything once I was in the saddle. No one cared. No one said, 'Ah, poor short-legged bugger, let's give the little bastard a hand.'

Once we had all the body armour and battle helmets in place they simply jumped on their machines and roared away down the road.

I followed tentatively, not having ridden a manual-geared machine for some 50 years. They had not changed a lot in that time. I had trouble finding the right gear, stalled the thing several times, and grew very frustrated with myself. The problem was with my short legs: every time I stopped I simply fell over to one side. The bike was extremely heavy and it took all my meagre strength to right it. My arms grew more and more tired with every halt. I was holding the others up and that made me and them unhappy. They wanted to be haring down green lanes chucking up divots of mud. I wanted to be home in bed.

I did start getting to grips with the demon machine after several miles of tarmac. Then we turned off onto a bridleway, footpath, or something of that nature. Very narrow, very muddy (it had of course started to rain) and with a startling number of solid looking trees lining the route. Everyone else let out a joyous shout (including John) and tore off in a long line spraying the hedgerows with sludge. I brought up the rear, along with one of the biker-tutors, who kept urging me to 'Get yer cheeks off the saddle mate and stand up on the pegs'.

Flying down that lane was like running a gauntlet. Overhanging branches turned into whips, which lashed my face and body. The bends were hairpin and I kept expecting to meet terrified old ladies walking their terriers around each corner. Mud everywhere, sometimes so deep it was up to the wheel hubs. Water by the gallon, spraying the county of Hertfordshire willy-nilly. John came off and damaged his chest. I came off but managed to land in mud, so walked away unhurt. One of the other riders, an ex-policeman, came off and broke his wrist. I was amazed that there were no fatalities at the end of the day. And even more amazing, they all enjoyed it! For myself, it was the best experience of my life, and the worst. I had no desire to repeat it. Seven hours of battling through swamp and bog, hemmed in on all sides by trees, with the occasional rock thrown in, is not really my idea of fun.

I did think, at the end of the day, while I was driving home to Suffolk with my limbs aching and my eyes half-closed, that the Australian Outback would not, could not, be as challenging as that day on the dirt trails of Hertfordshire. After all, it didn't rain in the Outback, did it? No mud then. And there were only bushes in the bush, weren't there? No damn solid-trunked trees to worry about then. And I would be riding a small machine, one which would allow short-asses like me to touch the ground with their toes on both sides at once.

Little did I know at the time that there would be other obstacles, just as formidable, perhaps even more so, out in Ozzie walkabout country, where the horizons are further away than infinity.

True, we would get no rain.

I have known biblical deluges in my time.

Once, on a backpacking holiday with friends Rob and Sarah, the Malaysian rain came down in barrels. We were on a windowless bus crossing the central jungle and came to a river where a bridge had been washed away. Night fell, black as the deepest cave. With torches we had to cross on bendy planks that threatened to throw us into the swirling torrent below. Then, having escaped from a watery death we reached the coast to take deck passage on a fishing boat to Tioman Island. When we arrived at the island's jetty it was still monsoon rain. It bleached our skins and clothes. It washed our flight tickets and passports clean of any ink. Our backpacks were sodden lumps. The A-frame huts on the campsite leaked. It was the Ramadan month, so there was no fishing going on and consequently very little to eat. Now, my pal Rob is a big guy who likes his steak and ale. There was none of that. We stayed four days and then took a small plane back to the mainland, having survived on banana porridge and Fanta drinks. Only the magnificent Malaysian trees and wildlife saved it from being an absolute disaster.

3. PREPARATIONS

The official and rather posh title of the 2008 postie bike challenge was:
Brisbane to Cairns via the Gulf of Carpenteria
Previous years rides:
2002 and 2003 Brisbane to Darwin
2004 and 2005 Brisbane to Adelaide
2006   Brisbane to Alice Springs
At the time of writing I received an invitation to the newest route:
2009   Brisbane to Melbourne

What I should have done before jumping at the chance to ride through the Australian Outback was to look up the history of the ride, starting with the 2002 run. If had done, I would have found out some humbling facts which are only now evident to me while in the process of writing my small account of the 2008 ride. You will have noticed that this book is dedicated, among others, to the men who acted as volunteer mechanics during our ride. One of those men is simply referred to as 'Lang'. Well Lang Kidby OAM, father of Kylie one of the two organisers of the challenge, just happens to be an Australian hero, though you wouldn't have known it by the quiet way he went about fixing our bikes when they went wrong, and nudging us on when we got stuck on the trail and the several other duties he carried out.

Lang, along with his wife Bev, are Australian adventurers and have organised and led many expeditions through many countries, including Australian desert crossings, flights in antique planes, reconstructing a replica of a 1919 Vickers Vimy bomber and flying it from Australia to the UK, restoring a 1940 Dodge Army staff car and driving it from Aqaba to Paris and most significant of all, recreating the 1907 Peking to Paris motor race using restored cars from the period, Lang and Bev driving a 1907 ITALA. This man plotted the centre of Australia and was the recipient of the Medal of the Order of Australia. He has led military and civilian expeditions through jungles and was an army pilot with the Aviation Corps for 14 years.

They don't come any bigger or more modest than Lang Kidby.

Lang and Hans Tholstrup (another Aussie adventurer - the country is crawling with them) organised the first Postie Bike Challenge in 2002, a job he has since handed over to his daughter and her partner. He now travels with the team as one of the mechs and helpers.

Looking up that first ride I came up with a news report from ABC News Online, which might have made me wonder if Pete was hauling me into something that was well out of my comfort zone:

Quote: *The 2002 Postie Bike Challenge organised by adventurers Hans Tholstrup and Lang Kidby has proven too challenging for some. The 4000 km charity ride split at Julia Creek yesterday when more than a quarter of the 80 riders decided* **the dirt roads through the Gulf** *were too gruelling. So far 7 participants have withdrawn with head injuries, broken collarbones and broken ankles. One of the riders says his experience as a (real) postie has helped only slightly.* Unquote.

I'm glad I didn't see this article before my ride, knowing we were also going on the dirt roads through the Gulf. It probably wouldn't have stopped me going, but it would have made me that much more nervous. I'm also glad I didn't then know Lang's amazing history. I would have pestered him like a Melbourne fly and annoyed the hell out of him. I did manage to annoy his daughter. I had failed to get two of the ride t-shirts at the outset and Kylie ordered me some more. I asked her one too many times whether they had arrived. Kylie had a lot more to worry about than items of clothing for a 67 year old hack.

In August, a month before the ride, Pete sent me a list of the things I would need. However, everything had to go into a soldier's kitbag. It wasn't a big kitbag and it had to hold a tent, air bed, pump and sleeping bag, as well as the following items:

sunnies (Strine for sunglasses)
bandanna (to prevent choking on red dust)
thongs (Strine for flip-flops)
calculator
head torch
2 fibre t-shirts
light shoes
bathers
washable long trousers
light socks
swiss army knife
camping towel
camping pillow (mistake, didn't work)
soap
pens
notebook
camera
spare batteries
toothbrush and paste
Vaseline (oh the relief after a day in the saddle!)
camera and spare battery/charger
sandals
sunscreen
paracetamol
ear plugs (against snorers, of which there were many)
washing powder and pegs
water camel (threw this away after the first day)
cap

mobile phone (turned out to be useless in the Outback - no coverage)
jeans
jumper

It was, as you might imagine, a hellava struggle to get it all in. I saw guys jumping on their bags to get the stuff to stay put. Fortunately the zips were strong and once you wrestled the contents to the ground, you zipped up the bag quickly before everything kicked out again and sprayed the campsite with underwear and toothbrushes.

On the first day of September, Annette and I boarded a Royal Brunei flight for Brisbane, Australia. There were two stop-offs, one of an hour at Dubai where we were supposed to disembark and buy buckets of gold jewellery. The other was for three hours at Brunei, which had an airport lounge not much bigger than my kitchen. The economy flight was tedious and uncomfortable. We have done it several times before and each time it seems longer and more unbearable. Always, just as I manage to fall asleep in a contorted sideways knot, the guy behind stands using the back of my seat to pull himself upright, thereby joggling me instantly awake. I usually glare at him, but find he's lost somewhere in his own head and has no idea that I live on the periphery of his world. The only thing I can say about modern aeroplane flights to Oz is that they're probably better than the old three months at sea playing deck quoits and canasta until one is sick of one's neighbours, sick of the colour green, and sick of being sick during the occasional storm.

Even short voyages by sea are to be avoided.

Annette and I were once on our way to Rhodes, when there was a terrible a storm in the Med. We were on board a Greek car ferry which had been a French battleship during WW1. The vessel was still painted navy grey and all the embossed metal signs above doors and gangways were still in French. Our new Volkswagen beetle was strapped to the deck as the world began to rise and heave all around us.

The kids were still young then - Chantelle 6, and Richard 8 - and we had a cabin in the depths of the ship adjacent to an empty hold. Someone had forgotten to batten down a giant crane hook dangling on a chain as thick as my thigh. The hook itself was the size of a railway truck. It swung back and forth in the storm clanging monstrously on the side of our cabin, knocking the kids out of their bunks. We were not en-suite and every time someone wanted to go the toilet (which was fairly often, given the conditions) they had to accurately time their run across the void which was the ship's hold, or become a fly-smudge on one of the iron walls of the vessel.

We thought we were going to die during that storm, which lasted for 24 hours. Every time the ship's bow went down under the water, we were convinced it would never rise again. I vowed then that I would only ever get on another boat in a dire emergency.

On arrival at Brisbane, we took a taxi to our accommodation, the local Quaker Meeting House. Annette and I are Quakers and we are much more comfortable in a bed-and-breakfast environment than in a luxury hotel. It's not that we scorn luxury, or consider it decadent, but would much rather be in a room with breathable, unrecycled air. We both find the atmosphere in modern hotels oppressive and though the breakfasts are enough to feed one for the whole day, there is a kind of suppressed panic in the dining room as people form in small bunches around the multi-slice toaster to anxiously watch their personal bit of bread disappearing inside the machine, terrified they will be unable to identify it when it drops out as toast into the tray beneath.

The Brisbane Quaker Meeting House was on the steepest hill I've ever seen covered in tarmac. Walking down it was a frightening experience. One felt it would be so easy to lean forward, then topple the rest of the way down that sheer black surface. The house itself though was in a beautiful forested garden. It was the Aussie Spring and we woke the next morning to a chorus of bell birds, butcher birds and kookaburras. The latter of course do not have melodic calls, but certainly the bell bird with its flute-like chimes and the butcher birds with their variety of warbled notes were gentle alarm clocks.

We had a free day so we went into Brisbane proper, walked along Queen Street and Elizabeth Street, and visited the Brisbane's City Hall, with its wonderful clock tower. Brisbane is named after Sir Thomas Brisbane, an 18th Century general. He was one of those rugged soldiers who probably *asked* for a posting to a rugged land. His military career is in the Guinness Book Of Records as being the longest. Our Tom apparently served 70 years in the army and he was famous for having slept six nights in continental winter snows with nothing but his cloak to keep him warm. Each morning he found himself frozen hard to the ground, while around him in the night many common soldiers had died with the cold. They don't make generals like that these days, though when I was in Aden during violent times, I did hear of a general who put up with chilly air-conditioning without a murmur of complaint.

After City Hall, we visited the United Church, just off Albert Street, where a Japanese couple was getting married. We sat in a pew at the back and watched the ceremony. The church was empty. There were no guests, no attendees. Just the wedding couple. They went the whole hog with music, a choir singing, she in full white wedding dress, he in tuxedo and top hat. A photographer, of course. But no friends or relatives. When we asked the registrar after it was all over, what was happening, she told us it was a common occurrence. They married in Japan then came to Australia to have another wedding, simply to gather photographs and videos of the ceremony. It was then I remembered seeing the same thing in Venice. There an Asian couple had changed clothes behind a billboard, he had set up a camera on the steps of a church with St Mark's Square in the background, and they had then posed in their wedding kit for a series of self-taken photos.

How strange this world has become since my grandparents shuffled off their mortal coils.

While in Brisbane we went to stay with Dave and Doreen, great friends of my brother. They showed us the Glasshouse Mountains, so called because one of the first Poms, Captain Cook, thought they looked like the glass-blowing factories of Northern England. Dave and Doreen's house is actually owned by a dog called Chewbacca, a lovely border collie. Chewbacca lets the couple live there free of rent. Chewbacca actually wanted one of those Queenslander dwellings that look like the southern USA mansion in *Gone With The Wind*, but he had to settle for a less expensive single-storey ranch-style dwelling.

Next, we went north, to Noosa Heads for the day. Richard Branson was a frequent visitor at Noosa, where he used to go running early morning. The story is that he liked a cold fruit juice after his run and finding no juice bar open at that time of the morning he purchased one of his own which he opened at six in the morning.

On the 4th day we went back to Brisbane. I dressed in my biker gear - big boots, armoured jacket, knee guards, motocross jeans, reinforced gloves and big black motocross helmet - and went to find the rallying point for the bikers. We had been told it was at the Exhibition Grounds. Annette and I lugged my army-style kitbag through streets broad and narrow, going from one Exhibition site to another. In Brisbane they cover a vast area and I was looking for a garage or hangar of sorts big enough to house fifty motorbikes and their riders. Eventually I rang Dan on the mobile and he guided me along a street I had passed twice already. What hope did I stand in the Outback?

I met Pete and John just entering the building.

'You found it then?' said Pete. 'Didn't get lost?'

'What, me?' I laughed gaily. 'I'm a walking compass.'

We entered a warehouse humming with people, some in motorcycle gear, others in street clothes. There were lots of beards about, several of them quite long, mostly grey and grizzly. Most of the people in the room were men between the ages of 25 and 75, but I was surprised by the number of them in their 40's and 50's. They were all roaming around identical bright red motorcycles, which peppered the floor looking clean and shiny. These roadsters were being inspected and appraised by their new owners. To some of those owners these small postie bikes were tiddlers, but to me they were mean machines.

The dominant accent that echoed around this hollow room was naturally Australian. Some people knew each other, but most did not, and the beginnings of camaraderie were emerging as strangers spoke to each other about the coming enterprise:

'Hi, I'm Dave. Up from Sydney. You?'

'Bill - you up for this?'

'Hope so. Been looking forward to it.'

'Me too.'

All very gentle and tentative. Later they would be greeting each other in the mornings with a slap on the shoulder and something like:

'Bill, you crusty old bastard. There's a rumour you came in last yesterday.'

'Not a chance, mate. The day you don't cough on my dust ain't arrived yet.'

'Yeah, right.'

I went to meet the organiser, Dan Gridley.

Dan was a man of good build, neat of dress, and you could tell he had an underlying seam of toughness. Kylie, his partner and helper, was pretty and a very good organiser. Dan showed me my bike, Number 21 in red figures on the headlamp, and left me to learn from others how to pack the milk crate which would carry essentials like petrol, water, food and other bits and pieces. The crate fitted on the back of the bike and Pete had made covers for all three crates. He had also brought elastic ties to keep the lid down on rough ground. In fact, I was being babied quite a lot: something that would soon change.

Dan gave us our briefing for Sunday's departure.

'I want you here, ready to leave at 7 o'clock tomorrow morning. We'll all leave the city together. There was going to be a police escort, but they're busy with road runs and other events . . .' He then told us how a normal day would go once we were out of the city. 'We usually rise about 5.30 am, pack up our tents and then have breakfast. The night before you will have checked your bike for any problems, filled your spare gas tank with fuel, lubricated your chains and made sure there's no slack there, and checked your oil levels.

'Departure is around seven every morning, after a daily briefing. The first to leave will be the marker truck, which will tie coloured tape to key points along the route, so you'll know where and when to make a turn. Your bags will be carried by the repair truck, and a sweeper truck will follow behind all the riders, helping those in trouble. You'll be expected to do your own repairs where possible. Tools can be borrowed from the repair truck. If you can't do it, because it's too technical or you need muscle assistance, Richard, Lang, Andy or Mick will be there to help or take over. When you arrive at the campsite in the evening - usually a town showground or rodeo ground - the first thing you'll do is check your bike for potential problems, oil and lube, and refuel. Then put up your one-man tents and finally, get a beer.

'Any questions?'

I had no idea what to ask, so I said nothing.

My bike looked young and fresh, despite having 30-odd thousand kilometres on the clock. As postie bikes they all looked exactly alike of course. Little robust-looking Honda 110s, designed for 'commercial and agricultural use'. The 'X' model, which we were using, had a reliable four-stroke engine and was simple and undemanding. Although it had 4-speed gearbox, it was what we call in England a 'semi-automatic'. There was no clutch. You crunched through the gears from neutral upwards, 1 through to 4, and so on, down again. We were given a lesson in first-line maintenance by Richard, Mick and Andy, three of the mechanics who were to accompany us. Checking the oil level and tyre pressures every day was a must. Watching for looseness of chain and any nuts and bolts was also important. Pretty trivial stuff, I thought.

(That was until we were hammering along the wild trails of untamed Northern Queensland. Two-hundred or so kilometres of brick-hard corrugated track, rugged enough to shake loose the teeth of saltwater croc, soon changed my mind about 'trivialities'.)

'These'll save you some cramped fingers,' Pete said, giving me some soft grips for the handlebars. 'After steering for seven hours, your fingers will be like claws on those hard grips.'

I duly cut away the hard grips and replaced them with soft spongy ones that did indeed make my life a lot easier on the trail.

Kick-starting my lovely 21 for the first time, she sounded, as another rider remarked, like a cross between a lawn mower and portable generator. The sort of noise that causes the dead to spin in their graves. Spanish youths use similar machines to ride up and down the same stretch of road carrying half-a-dozen of their mates on the frame and mudguards, while holiday-makers vainly attempt to rest.

On the back of the bike was a plastic milk crate. Pete had made me a cover for it and had provided some elastic retainers to keep it on. In our milk crates we would carry 5 litres of fuel, 2 litres of water, sandwiches, a thick book of maps covering the vast and seemingly empty interior of a continent (most of the pages looked blank to me) and 'personal materials'.

My personal items consisted of two toilet rolls, a packet of cleansing wipes, imodium tablets, and dehydration powders (blackcurrant flavour). Add to these essentials a brass naval compass and it can be seen that my major fears were divided equally between loose bowels and getting lost in the wilderness.

As it happened the former was to become reality and the latter was to remain a harrowing nightmare.

When I was 12 years of age I got lost, with another boy scout, for two days in a South Arabian desert. The maps given to us were later proved to be faulty. Such experiences don't leave your mind, even after 55 years. Horrific tales, which we have all heard, of people wandering away from their car to take a pee in the Outback, never to be seen again, haunted my early thoughts on the trip. I was almost persuaded into purchasing a hand-gps system. I had visions of myself drinking the petrol out of my fuel tank while the mystical landscape of the Aborigines swam around me distorted by heatwaves. In the end cost got the better of my fears. I settled for a good compass. I figured a gps would only tell me where I was, i.e. lost in the Outback.

By the end of the day, armed with information and items to stay alive and moving on two wheels, I went back to my Quaker accommodation somewhat uneasy with my inexperience. Would I manage to ride this sturdy little machine without falling off? Would I manage to travel the hinterland of Australia without getting lost? Would I manage to complete the trip without getting 'crook'?

The answer to all these questions was actually, 'No'.

Here's a few statistics for the bike nerds amongst you, on the Honda CT-110 Postie Bike, so that you are fully aware of what our multi-national bums were about to sit astride.

Dry Weight:	89.5 kg (197 lb)
Engine Oil:	1.1 L (1.2 US qt)
Fuel Tank:	5.5 L (1.4 US gal)
Fuel Reserve:	0.8 L (0.2 US gal)
Forks:	140 ml (4.7 oz)
Bore & Stroke:	53 mm x49.5 mm (2.047 x 1.948 in)
Compression Ratio	8.5:1
Displacement:	105.1 cm3 (6.39 cu.in)
Spark Plug:	D8EA (NGK)
Spark Plug Gap:	0.6 - 0.7 mm (0.024-0.028 in)
Ignition:	CDI
Points Gap:	0.3-0.4 mm (0.012-0.016 in)
Valve Clearance:	0.05 mm (0.002 in) both
Idle Speed:	1,500 + or - 100 rpm
Output Power	7.5 HP(DIN) @ 7,500 rpm
Clutch:	Wet plate (semi-automatic or crunch gear)
Gear Box:	4-speed

Stroke:	4-stroke
Top Speed	85 kph

Soichiro Honda set up the Honda company in October 1945. The war had not long been over and he used military 2-stroke motors that he purchased cheaply. When they ran out he designed his own 50cc engine. In 1958 he released the C100 Super Cub, a 4-stroke, overhead valve motor, with a centrifugal clutch and 3-speed gearbox. 70cc and 90cc versions followed a bit later. Honda has since sold close to 40 million of these bikes, which includes the Postie Bike, one of the toughest machines on the road. I was soon to learn that the CT-110 needed to be a robust worker, to deal with conditions out in the wilds of Australia. Corrugated roads, thick bull dust, heat, up to 8 continual hours a day at almost top speed, rocks, gravel, sand and a novice rider - all these my little bike took in its stride - and never once did it falter or even look like giving up.

So, there were 50 of these magnificent little colts with a rider on each one of them, but the organisers were carrying 6 spare bikes on one of the three trucks, just in case. It turned out they knew what they were doing, naturally, because I think they eventually used all six.

PART TWO

DAY ONE

I rose at 5.30 and dressed in my road armour: helmet, boots, shoulder and elbow protectors, and shin and kneecap guards. Then I kissed Annette goodbye (she opened one eye, briefly) and then went to the start point of the rally. Fifty riders and fifty postie motorbikes. A couple of Americans, a few Brits, several New Zealanders, and naturally in the great majority, Australians. Mostly men, but also a handful of women. One of the women, a good-looking lass, was wearing the full body armour of Boudicca, the Celtic warrior Queen who thundered around in a chariot killing Romans right, left and centre, in BC Britain. Most impressive. I was envious. With armour like that who cared whether you came off the bike and bounced around a bit?

'Howya doin'?' asked a lazy-eyed, dark-haired Aussie about half my age, as I wheeled the bike out. 'You up for it?'

'As I'll ever be,' I replied. 'You?'

'No worries,' he came back with the traditional Oz reply, and gave me the broad grin of a rider who knew what he was doing.

I was actually quite nervous. I'd only had about 20 hours riding in my whole life, all on borrowed motorcycles. Nothing came automatically to me. I could drive a car without even thinking, had been doing for 50 years. Now I had to think 'throttle', think 'brake, where is it, which one?', think 'gears, where are they, what am I supposed to be in?', think 'lifesaving look over left shoulder for turning left, over right shoulder for turning right' and a dozen other things.

They did not just happen in any natural way. I had to *think* about them and think quickly. Nothing was instinctive.

So of course I was nervous.

I didn't want to make an ass of myself on the first day. I didn't want to make an ass of myself on *any* day, of course, but I knew I was going to at some time, so begged it would not be just as we started out. I didn't want to be the butt of jokes or the one they picked out as the dodo from amongst all these Kiwis, Yanks, Ozzies and Poms. We lined up two abreast. A long line, stretching back the length of the sideroad. One support truck was in the lead and another followed, with two others somewhere around. There was supposed to be a police escort out of the City of Brisbane, but other things were going on too. A charity run for a start. We had lost our motorbike escort to the Heart Foundation.

'Start up!' came the call down the line.

Please start, please start. One kick and 21 roared to life, the little darling. Gear up into first and we were away. The line broke up fairly soon afterwards, both longwise and sidewise. We went out as a trickle, finding our way through the Sunday morning traffic to the outer reaches of the city. It was a fairly straight route, for which I was thankful. Getting lost in the Outback actually held fewer fears than getting lost in the city. In the Outback there was only kangaroos and the very occasional road train to worry about. Here in the city was mindless traffic and a multitude of unfathomable roads.

Those on their way to churches and/or pubs on that Sunday gave us a good hooting send off. It must have been something to see 50 postie motorbikes scrambling along the highway. One of us, Scotty, was dressed in a clown's outfit, wig on top of his helmet. Why? Only Scotty knew. 'It seemed like the thing to do,' he told me later, when I asked if it was a bet or charity stunt. 'I just felt I needed to do it.' Scotty was an expert mechanic and of great assistance to those who broke down when the repair truck was nowhere in sight. There were others with similar skills. What had I got to offer? I could write them a poem, of course, on the wonderful song of the Australian bell bird or the absurdity of the duckbilled platypus, but somehow I didn't see that helping.

(I remember a writer friend of mine, who when he obtained his doctorate in literature from Canterbury University saying he longed to be in a theatre when someone fell ill. When the call came out, 'Is there a doctor in the house?' he planned to rush forward and cry, 'Yes, stand back while I read the patient a couple of verses from Shelley.')

I was not wearing my goggles at this point. Only prescription aviator sunglasses, or 'sunnies' as the Ozzies call them. The goggles would not go on over my glasses, which I needed in order to see properly. Later, after several stone chips had nearly taken my lenses out, I forced the damn goggles over the glasses. They were uncomfortable but absolutely necessary. The weather was good. It had been raining hard when we arrived in Brisbane. Torrents, accompanied by an earthy, rainforesty smell. People had been getting onto buses and trains and emptying pints of water out of their shoes. But the rain had passed and it was a mild and pleasant spring day in Southern Queensland.

Dayglow youngsters roared past me, occasionally whooping and hollering, giving release to their feelings. They rode their bikes like young Mongols rode wild horses, following some invisible Ghengis Khan. Others, the middle-aged and older men were more sedate, but still highly competent. I clung grimly to my handlebars, mentally mumbling, 'Change down to 3rd. Shit, I'm already in 3rd' as I slowed almost to a stop. 'OK, get a grip. Think about what you're doing. No, don't touch the front brake, use your back foot brake you idiot or you'll be sailing over the handlebars. Whoa, miss that bus if you please, Mr Kilworth. Don't wanna join the insects on the windscreen. Change up again, and again, heck there is no *again*, I'm already in 4th. Well at least I know where I am now, but for how long, god only knows and he's a secretive little . . . heck, that engine noise gets my tinitus going, but don't think about that, or the slight headache, think about what you're doing, or you'll oversteer. Look ahead, not down. Look right ahead, way, way ahead, so far ahead you'll be staring over the world's edge.'

Taped to my handlebars was my Running Sheet, which told me where to turn and when. I began the day at 36,862 kms and from that point all the way down a numbered sheet had worked out what my speedo should read when deviating from the straight and narrow. At 36,908 I needed to turn right to **Esk, Brisbane Valley Highway #17 - CAUTION! Crossing duel carriageway.** I followed the instructions, along with 50 others. There would be times when I would be alone in the world and these sheets would save my bacon. Today the destination was a town called Gayndah, northwest of Brisbane. Today's fuel stop, where we would refill our spare tank and top up the tank on the bike, was **Jimna Fire Tower**, in a lightly forested region with a gravel road.

At 37,1018 we forked left to Jimna and there rested in a dirt layby by a 47 metre high tower from which rangers presumably watched for forest fires. After scoffing sandwiches and drinking water, I put on my motocross helmet back on. We were going onto gravel now, obviously more dangerous than bitumen, and Pete had suggested John and I followed him, did what he did, went at the same speed. After two minutes it seemed not so much gravel as hard dirt with lots of potholes and rocks sticking up. I tried to keep up with Pete's 70 kph but was worried about the sticky-up rocks, so slowed a little to about 65 kph. Pete slowed too, to keep me and John company.

The track was undulating, with some fairly steep slopes and rises. We turned one corner, started to go down a descent when we noticed a knot of bikes and riders on the edge of the forest road. Someone had come off. More than one person. It seemed a jam so we didn't stop ourselves. We'd only be adding to the clog-up. In fact we later learned that a rider had gone over the edge, into a culvert (I'd never heard of a culvert until that day) which is a kind of channel or watercourse alongside a road. The rider, a guy named Jack, had several broken ribs and facial injuries. Cuts and bruises too. At 75 Jack was the oldest one amongst us. Next oldest was a Kiwi, at 70-odd, then me at 67. I hoped the Biker Gods weren't starting at the oldest and working their way down. Jack then was out of the rally and was whisked away in an ambulance. As someone remarked, you don't bounce at that age.

Someone else had run into Jack from behind, when the accident happened, but I never found out who. Pete started to speed up after that and I actually passed him on this occasion. It was probably the only time I did while on dirt, but I felt quite good. We finished with the 'gravel' and once again went onto bitumen, or what I would call in UK tarmac. The next name on our sheet was Ban Ban Springs, on the Goomeri road.

Ban Ban Springs are a line of natural springs at the end of the Bin Bin Range of hills (dontcha just love these Aboriginal place names?) the water of which runs into wetlands covered with wildlife and plants. The springs were a source of water for the Aborigine clans of the region, a sacred place with Dreamtime associations with the Rainbow Serpent. It is the birthplace of the Wakka Wakka tribe. It's one of those areas, apparently, where one should stop, relax, and contemplate the serenity of nature. Unfortunately, blokes and gals zooming along on 70 kph bikes don't have time to stop and lay out a picnic blanket, then muse on the wonders of the natural world.

We hurtled past.

Goomeri, on the other hand, is famous for its Maytime Pumpkin Festival, which attracts thousands of people to the small town. Apparently the Great Australian Pumpkin Roll has made Goomeri internationally famous. It sounded very inviting but again, bike riders are obsessed with 'getting there' and we wanted to reach our destination at Gayndah before nightfall. 377km in total. A longish day.

On the way I saw my first Whistling Kite, a beautiful bird of prey that skimmed the treetops.

Also saw a kookaburra on a wire. He laughed at me. Why wouldn't he?

At Gayndah we camped in the local showground where I put up my one-man tent for the first time. It was simple and easy. Went up in ten minutes. Blew up the bed, unrolled the sleeping bag. Went for a shower, thence for a drink at the make-shift bar. Pete was leaning on a fence talking into his mobile phone. He used his hands for emphasis, despite the fact that the caller could not see him. Behind this darkening silhouette of a white-bearded Melbournian, along an immense horizon, was the most multi-hued sunset I'd ever seen. It stained the landscape red, orange, purple and mauve. Breathtaking. First day over and I had covered it pretty well. I felt good. This was cool stuff. No worries. Pete and John had beers, I had a Tennessee whisky-and-coke. Pretty soon the night sky stretched itself over us, smothered in unfamiliar stars. I sought that diamond symbol of Australia in the sky, the Southern Cross, and found it safely embedded in the sky amongst its fellows. The air was as clear as crystal. This was not yet the Outback. Pete reckoned the Outback began where fences ceased to be. We still had fences.

The Queensland Country Women's Association (founded in 1922 for women who derived their living from the land) cooked us an evening meal which was delicious. I can't remember what it was, but every meal we had on that ride was good and most of them were provided by the charitable QCWA. Wonderful ladies. The lunchtime sandwiches were something else, being sliced white bread smothered in marg, with processed meat innards. But heck if you've got a good breakfast inside you, eggs, bacon, beans and sausage, and you're looking forward to a great dinner, what do you need lunch for? And what else were they to do? The fresh fruit and cake went down well, that's for sure, while the kangaroos and kookaburras often got the sandwiches.

Gayndah, what we saw of it, was a pleasant town. The spot was discovered by a Henry Stuart Russell in 1843. He saw the River Burnett (named later) and thought the land around it looked fertile. Gayndah claims to be the oldest town in Queensland, Ipswich and Brisbane being cities. In Gayndah oranges *are* the only fruit. They grow the best oranges in the world, dontcha know. They also host a local Bush Poets Competition. I wanted to stay and take part in it, this being my forte rather than biking, but I was called to my bed by an overwhelming tiredness at 8 pm.

Anyway, I told myself, as I sped along a whitelined highway in my dreams, what did I know about the bush? It's all very well being a poet, but that was only half the job. You need a special wilderness touch to write twangy Oz poems like 'Nine Miles from Gundagai' by Bowyan Yorke.

'There goes Bill the Bullocky,

He's bound for Gundagai . . .

Never earnt an honest crust . . .

Never drug a whip through dust.'

(carries great alliteration in its stride, finishing with)

'. . . the dog sat on the tucker box,

Nine miles from Gundagai.'

Forget your prissy 'O daffodils we weep to see thee fade away so soon'. Bush poems have a good hard outbacky feel to them with words like 'Murrumbidgee' appearing in the middle of the verse. Nothing too fancy. Nothing too airy-fairy. Just good solid verse with a story to it, a beginning and end. This is Australian history, where a dog eats a bullock cart driver's tucker while he's away having an honest drink. I like Oz poetry, just as I'd liked the poems of Robert Service when I visited the Yukon in Canada. Poems like 'The Shooting of Dan McGrew'. You don't write poems like that by growing up fancy. You have to be as hard as a bullet and eat gravel for breakfast. Who says it's not poetry? A poem, like any art, is what touches the heart of the beholder.

Next morning, up at 5 am.

Pack away the tent, fold up the sleeping bag, get a fatter neighbour to roll over and over your inflatable mattress to try to get it flat again (you can never quite get rid of all the air, can you, just as dirt from a hole never quite fills it when you put it back - ah the mystery of physics - it was ever thus at school). Cram everything in the kitbag and throw the bag onto the sweeper truck. Go for breakfast, collect those astonishing sandwiches, and then gather round Dan-the-man for the day's briefing. Everyone looks eager to go. Many riders want dust or gravel, preferably with lots of curves and ups-and-downs but most of today is bitumen.

I'm quite happy with tarmac at the moment.

4. DAY TWO

I remember that morning vividly. It wasn't the Outback, there were still fences, but the landscape opened up like untying a brown parcel. It became immense. Even though 50 riders started off almost together, we soon became strung out. There were younger more vigorous riders who wanted to burn it up out front. There were those who wanted to dawdle and take photos of everything from yellow-flowering wattle trees to dead kangaroos. I sort of found myself in the middle. Mostly I stuck to Pete's tail, terrified I would get lost if I didn't. (It was bloody easy to miss those coloured ribbons marking our route). But on occasion I was the only person in a gigantic flat bushland. Solitary Max. It was quite cold early on, before the sun had warmed the world. The wind cut through me as I hurtled into it at 70 kms. I made a mental note to stuff newspaper down the front of my jacket.

This is what I had joined this rally for. Being alone in the Australian hinterland is indescribable. It's truly awe-inspiring, frightening in its immensity, and stunning in its aspect. I felt so very privileged to be able to experience such a scene. It drained me of all the bad feelings I had ever had. It filled me with wonder. My spirit expanded with the wide open wilderness as I hummed and rattled along the road, the bush stretching to infinity on either side, to back and to front. I was in the bubble of a sky the size of a universe. It was royal blue with puffs of cloud like the spots on a fallow deer's flanks. Except, down the centre of heaven was this long, long cloud, oh, a hundred kilometres long, under which I travelled most of the morning. Talk about white-line fever. I had one under me and one over me.

And crossing this rufous, sandy landscape horizontally, every half-hour or so, was a narrow creek. It might be CARVING KNIFE CREEK, or WOOMBA CREEK, or simply, JACK'S CREEK. Most had no water in them. One or two did. The trees around waterholes hid kangaroos and other wildlife. But I have to say most of the roos I saw were road kills, that threw up an unholy stink from their open-vault graves. No doubt they'd been hit by road trains, trucks or big cars. Unlike the rabbits or crows of England, they didn't flatten. If they were actually on the tarmac their bloated forms looked like hot-air balloons. I swerved round them, disturbing a thousand flies. Some of them were meals for the carrion-eating whistling kites, that soared overhead.

Today we started out towards Mundubbera, heading first towards Cracow. I saw a twelve-inch blue-tongued lizard crossing the road in front of me: lovely creature. Around me the bush, with the occasional shrub, dwarf tree, or rocky outcrop. The noise from my bike engine was excruciating after a while. It grated on the nerves and I realised why a lot of the lads wore earplugs. Also my riding gear was uncomfortable. The goggles pressed my glasses into the bridge of my nose. Flies got inside the helmet and drove me insane. I itched in various places. My bum got sore after two hours. My teeth rattled along with the loose bits of metal on the bike frame. When I hit a bump in the road the jolt went right up my spine and kicked my cerebellum like a football. The scenery was magnificent. The method of viewing it less so.

That last evening one of the Ozzie biker boys had sat down next to me after the meal and had started to talk bikes. Pistons, drive-chains, cooling ribs, fairings, etc., etc. He might have been speaking in the tongues of angels, so far as I was aware. My eyes glazed over after five minutes, though I listened politely for half-an-hour before saying, 'Look mate, I appreciate your enthusiasm, but I'm not a biker. I'm on this trip for other reasons.' He stared at me in a puzzled way for a minute or two, then said, 'Yeah, OK, mate . . .' then carried on for the next hour-and-a-half in the same vein as before, without pause for breath.

If I knew nothing about bikes when he'd started his talk, I knew even less about them at the end, realising as one does, how complex and intricate was this holy subject, and how utterly confused I was by it. I knew where the gear lever was (quite a lot of the time actually) and the rear brake (when I remembered it wasn't on the handlebars, like the front brake) and a few of the little switches like the fuel switch and cut-out switch, oh, and the bung hole where you top up with oil, but as to what lay beneath the cladding, that was still a occidental secret. I could lube my chain, refill my fuel tank, put air in the tyres, check the oil, start and stop the machine (with only occasional hiccups) and that was good enough for the run we were on. If anything else went wrong I ran to Richard-the-mechanic and started to cry. Richard is one of those unsung geniuses who know everything about bikes and probably bikers, has taught kings and princes the fundamentals of bike maintenance, and who never ever reveals his disdain for idiots like me. When fixing whatever it was that had gone wrong he always told me what he was doing, why he was doing it, and what the end product should be.

Miraculously I absorbed these snippets of knowledge so that next time I could fix the same problem myself.

The run to Cracow was just short of 200 kms, some of it over gravel roads which required a certain amount of respect.

In a roadside café, many of us were sipping coffee, dressed in our biker gear, with the robust red Honda Postie Bikes propped up in a neat row in the parking lane outside. A little old lady of the Outback entered and stared around with saucer eyes at the luminous-jacketed riders.

'My goodness,' she said, 'what are all you posties doing out here?'

One of the guys, on his way to the exit, said firmly, 'Step aside if you please, madam - the mail must get through.'

We laughed then let her in on the secret. She laughed with us.

At another place, a real postie joined the end of our straggling line of machines, staying with us for a couple of kilometres, before turning off on a farm track and waving a cheery goodbye.

Cracow is an ex-gold-mining town in the unlikely named Banana Shire area. Cracow was obviously named after the Polish city with a different spelling. All we saw of this ghost town was the Cracow Hotel, which is owned by a guy called Fred Brophy, a famous bush boxing manager. The large bar inside the hotel (which looks a bit like a giant clapboard shack) is crammed with artefacts, from antlers to music boxes to worn saddles. It's an Aladdin's cave of junk that would send a Victorian era collector into shudders of ecstasy. Apparently tourists are attracted to the place, one of the reasons being there is probably no other watering hole in the district. I liked it. It has to be seen. We were told the first bit of gold to be found, back in the glory days of Cracow, was discovered by some wandering fossil hunters. Then another nugget was picked up by an Aborigine (who I hope made himself a rich man) and the subsequent mine was only closed down in 1976.

And so we thundered on towards the famous Banana itself, a small town named after a dun coloured bullock who lived and died there in the mid-1800s, a beast held in affection by the local stockmen who used old Banana to herd the wilder elements of their cattle into the stockyards. That's what you do in Oz. You don't have fancy Anglo-Saxon or Viking names for your towns. You name them after your favourite hound or work horse. And past Banana we went, with barely a backward glance, intent on reaching our goal which was the town of Rolleston over 200 kms away. We were staying at the Rolleston racecourse that night. My little motorbike was hot between my thighs and as we ate bitumen at the end of that day I recalled similar bikes and bikers I had seen in various parts of the world, especially on the Asian continent.

The small motorbike has been a great boon to the poorer areas of the world (some of them no longer so poor). I've spent a great deal of time in Malaysia, Thailand, Vietnam and other Asian countries and have witnessed some hair-raising small-motorbike-sights.

I remember once seeing two men riding in Ho Chi Min city. One guy was sitting on the saddle, head down, throttle open to the limit. His friend was standing on the pegs over the top of him. In the hands of the standing man was a huge pane of plate glass. His arms were stretched wide in the shape of a crucifix, his fingers hooked around the far edges of the glass. Around, in front, behind, and just about everywhere, were other bikes, cars, trucks - whizzing near this pair with only fractions of a inch to spare. I leave it to your own imagination how close these two came to death by multiple lacerations.

In another Far Eastern land, it was quite common to see a man sitting on a small motorbike with a live domestic beast sitting on the pillion seat, usually a pig, its front trotters tied together, its legs around the neck of the driver of the vehicle. It seemed never to bother either rider or passenger that they were cheek by jowl, the snout of the sow alongside the nose of the man. In fact it appeared to be the most natural thing in the world and I wonder if conversations were held between the two, one in animalese and the other in humanese. A grunt here, a snort there, an understanding developing over the journey to market.

By the afternoon we were still not in the Outback. I could see fences all around. There were irrigation channels too. Someone, Ewan I think, said he'd noticed cotton farming around the area. Ewan came from Darwin, so he knew the north well. He was a tall quietly-spoken man with 'Lonesome Rider' on his back. I liked him. There was no brashness or side about Ewan.

We refuelled at Theodore that day. Refuelling was done off the back of one of the trucks. You started out in the morning with 5 litres in the bike tank and five litres in the spare can. That would, in theory, take you 250 kms or more, depending on the rider's weight and how fast you pushed the bike along. Some days, like today, we had 450 kms to do. At the refuelling, usually midday or thereabouts, you took on another 10 litres and so could finish the journey comfortably.

In the afternoon we passed mining operations with trucks going back and forth. Otherwise it was endless road, going on to the edge of the world. I'm told that one of the riders, a guy named Cam, was attacked by a dog in Theodore town. Then in the afternoon a Jack Russell flew at him from out of nowhere. I noticed him around the Rolleston camp, later, with 'Two Dogs' written on his back. Cam must give off one of those atmospheres that drives dogs wild. Who knows, maybe he had some kangaroo dung on his boots?

There were two more casualties in camp. One of the women had fallen off her bike on the dirt road coming into the camp. Her leg was injured and the ambulance was called for. Also someone else was stretched out on his back, clearly in pain from that area. Two days and three casualties? Heck, at this rate would get through half our number before the ride was over.

There was a sheet we were supposed to sign when we arrived at our destination every day. It was a simple task, but one which I constantly failed at. As usual when I arrived at the camp that afternoon I forgot to sign the arrival sheet. I always forgot to sign it and in the end they got tired of bollocking me. My head was so full of long white clouds and distant horizons there was no room for ordinary things like the signing of sheets to confirm that I wasn't actually lost out in the wilderness, but here in camp humming a simple tune as I knocked in tent pegs one by one. Kylie must have got awfully tired of this Pom.

We had corned beef, cooked Aussie Outback style, for dinner, amongst a bunch of vegetables and bread. And pudding too. Followed by coffee or tea. It was clear from the start we weren't going to starve on this run. I had thought I might be able to lean down over the trip but the meals on those first two days soon put that wish back at the bottom of the well. I could just not eat so much, of course, which would do the trick, but damn me it would be a strong man who could resist that country cooking after a day in the saddle, yippy-ay-yay old buddy.

Everyone was getting to know each other a bit better by this second evening and exchanging stuff about home towns, home countries, home continents. The Aussies and the Kiwis got on best of course, and worst, just like rival neighbours anywhere. They reminded me of the English and Scots back home. When I see some Kiwis and Aussies sitting together, I just like to toss in the world 'rugby' or 'cricket' and watch as the temperature rises on both sides of the table. The Brits and the Yanks did not have the same ground to battle on. They don't play soccer or rugby and we don't play baseball or their football, so we ended up being awfully polite to one another, which was a bit tame. I went to look for Pete later, to have a talk about cricket. He was good for a blast at any time and would lambaste the English cricket team at the drop of an Akubra, while I - albeit with lesser ammunition - would have a good go at destroying the myth of Australian cricket domination.

I went to bed that night about 8.30, along with most of the camp. I woke again at about 11.30 and went to the toilet. It was dark over the camp site but there was one area where it was lit. Under a pool of light that fizzed with black clouds of flying insects the small team of mechanics were still hard at work. Richard, Lang, Mick and Andy were probably all there, tinkering away with problems we had given the machines during the day. I noticed a sad-looking bike with its guts strewn all over a slab of concrete flooring, the frame already thick with dirt. An autopsy. How the heck these metal surgeons put such dismembered bikes back together, all the bits in the right places, was beyond a mind like mine. This scene of engineering men - heads uncluttered by literary junk - toiling under late lamplights, righting mechanical wrongs, repeated itself over the next few nights.

It was of course a long way from the world of the wordsmith, this world of mechanics, though I too have laboured nights at getting the right line in the right place, turning a few jumbled words into a poem.

This was a vision of men who had made a modern day craft into an art. My work had never been good enough to cross boundaries like that. I could not turn an art into a useful thing: others took what I did and did that. They took my words and produced books. I have the greatest admiration for men like Lang who can rebuild antique aircraft and then have the guts to fly their recreations halfway round the world.

Men like Lang Kidby turn metal puzzles into actual shapes that one can not only touch and smell, see and hear, but that can *do* things like race along the road or fly in the air. I've written 80 novels and over 200 short stories, but they don't race and they don't fly, they don't do anything except sit there and wait to be read. As for engineering, if I can mend the toilet ballcock when it goes wrong (which I *can* do fellah) I congratulate the engineer in me. To understand the precision-made parts of a modern machine, to make an engine actually work, must be immensely satisfying. That kind of achievement is so far out of my mental territory it might as well be on the moon.

The blow-up pillow was useless, so I stuffed a sock bag with a towel and used that. It wasn't like home, but then nothing was. Indeed, I slept well until shocked awake by clanks and crashes. I sat bolt upright at 4 am thinking we'd been invaded and the tanks were breaking down the metal corrals. Then I remembered we were in the middle of Queensland and tanks would have job getting through the bull dust. It turned out to be a cattle station nearby, that was loading up its cattle B Doubles (articulated cattle trucks) ready for the day. What a racket! Had no one told them there were tired bikers in the next field? Would they have given a monkey's uncle if they had been told? Of course not. I managed to fall asleep again, but my dreams were full of sledgehammers.

5. DAY THREE

Chink, chink, rustle, chink. Somebody has obviously given up trying to sleep. They are up, pulling out pegs, wrapping their tent.

Pete grumbles, 'Is that you, Kilworth?'

'No.'

'What the hell are you doing? It's only four-thirty.'

'It's not me, I tell you. It's Wikipedia.'

Wikipedia is our name for a guy who is truly a carrier of knowledge, especially about the local wildlife. I'm always asking him questions. He knows about whistling kites and blue-tongued lizards. And many insects. Wikipedia is quietly getting his stuff together. Well, almost quietly. Just the occasional *chink* or *rustle*.

'It sounds like you.'

'Well it bloody well ain't.' Sound carries in a campsite.

John's voice. 'Is Garry getting up already?'

I give in. 'Yes, it's me - I'm getting up.'

The whole camp is stirring. Torch-lights are battling with the rising sun to see who can remain brightest longest. The torches lose of course. There's no beating the Ozzie sun once it's over the horizon. Most of the torches are of the headband kind. Miners' lamps. They leave your hands free for tasks. I climb into my riding gear, boots last. They're a pig to put on, the leather being stiff and unbending. They've lost their shine and are now thoroughly embedded with red and sandy-coloured dust. My plastic elbow guards, knee guards and bollock guards feel uncomfortable at first, but after half-an-hour I'm used to them. I trudge off, being ahead of the others in packing, and fetch three teas.

The shed where the breakfasts are being cooked is full of riders. Many have forgotten they've got a lit headband torch around their skull. Me included. They walk about, bemused, looking for the toaster. I get three paper cups full of tea and return to John and Pete. They are appreciative, which is something. John is a talker, bless him, and he talks while he's packing his bag. Pete screws up his eyes and looks at the new day as if it's challenging him to a duel.

We're almost ready for the road.

Once breakfast is over, the daily briefing from Dan is next on the agenda.

We left Rolleston, bound for Barcaldine. Today was all about bitumen. Tarmac from door to door. No dusty tracks. No interesting creeks to skid into. Just black tar and white lines.

Barcaldine is the town where the great shearers' strike took place in the late 1800s. I remember seeing a movie when I was a kid called 'The Shiralee' based on a novel by D'Arcy Niland, about a roving swaggie shearer and his child. *Shiralee* apparently means 'burden'. The burden is the young daughter the shearer has to drag around the sheep farms with him. I loved that film. It had great atmosphere. Whether it was accurate or not was irrelevant to me as a young boy. I wanted to be out there, on the dusty roads of Australia, in the Outback of Queensland. Now, here I was, heading for the heart of that shearing country, where shearers downed their clippers and told the establishment to go to hell, if for a short time only.

Barcaldine was an American bomber base during the war and has around 2000 souls today, one or two of whom apparently look north eastwards to the USA for their forebears. Pete, who did the ride in 2007 as well as 2008, told me how he had fared in that year. He had arrived in the town and asked for the oldest pub. Sent to a hostelry called 'The Artesian' he found he was a minor celebrity there amongst drinkers who were well into their favourite sport. They all had their photos taken with him, then he said he had to leave. A young woman tried to persuade him to stay, but he had to join the rest of the riders camping at the showgrounds and told her so. As he rode away she yelled after him, 'I'm only 30.' Despite the inferred offer he kept going.

On the way to Barcaldine we passed through Springsure and Emerald. There are precious stone mines at Emerald, but they don't mine emeralds there. The emerald the town is named after is a lush green hill at the back. What they mine at Emerald is sapphires. Not green stones, but blue. Most confusing. Apparently the sapphire fields at Emerald are the richest in the southern hemisphere. What is very interesting at Emerald is a tree that's 250 million years old. Happy Birthday, tree! It has now turned to stone, having fossilised, but still it's an impressive age. Dead though. The region is famous for its live plants too: sunflowers. A Van Gogh land of big blooms.

The journey that day was long and tedious, except for one incident when we were going across a creek. Pete was just in front of me. We were hammering away noisily at around 75 kph when this large kangaroo suddenly shot out of the bush and bounded across the road right in front of him. Pete didn't deviate, but I thought wow, that was close! Then a quick movement to my right made me turn my head. Another roo was leaping out of the undergrowth, this time towards me!. I braked sharply and skidded, while the kangaroo suddenly realised he was going to hit one of those many angry red machines that were careering through his territory. He did a quick sideways leap and then athletically spun round, turning back towards the way he had come. I missed his plumbob bottom by inches. Pete waved a hand over his shoulder as if to say, 'Pay attention, mate, or you'll end up as a kangaroo road kill.'

450 straight kilometres of bitumen is not great fun. Still, Pete entertained me at the stops with his dark tales of 'bull dust' trails to come. I would part company with my bike, he told me, everyone does. Secretly I thought: not me. I shall stay stuck to the saddle because I

shall be sensible and ride at a speed that will keep the bike firmly under my backside.

Little did I know.

Little did I understand the devious nature of bull dust.

Anyway, not today. Today we were cruising through greenish countryside, with kangaroo road kills every several miles. They were somewhat whiffy. I imagined the poor bastards being hit by a road train. Those big articulated monsters would mow them down as easily as a car going over a weasel. Bang. Squish. Kangaroo heaven. The kites were feeding though, and the ants, and various other beasties.

There are other road kills. Taipan snakes. Feral pigs.

'Anna has gone to the hospital,' one of the riders tells us as we stop for a coffee. 'She might be back, but maybe not.'

Anna was one of the female riders who had damaged her ankle when she parted company with her machine. That's two down so far. Maybe more. I had heard about someone whose back had gone, not from a fall but from a simple task like kick-starting the bike. My knees gripped the fuel tank of my lovely redheaded Honda beauty, with her hot vibrating flanks and willing chassis. We were not getting divorced if I could help it. Let no bull dust put us asunder. Till death us do part, I thought, hoping of course that it wouldn't come to *that*.

We entered Barcaldine by crossing a railway.

Railway journeys I have known.

My wife Annette and I were in Thailand in the late 1980's. We wanted to travel by train from Bangkok to Chang Mai on an overnight sleeper train. Just obtaining the ticket turned the clock back to a time when Rudyard Kipling was in his youth. First we obtained a number at a kiosk. We took that number, just a simple figure like 8 or 9, to an office where a man wrote our names in a great ledger. We then went to another office where we were assigned seats and canvas bunk beds that unrolled from the side of the carriage. Finally, we went to the last office, where we were issued with tickets for the 6 pm train to Chang Mai.

We were excited. This was our first long rail trip in the Far East.

At quarter-to-six that evening we boarded a train which said 'Bangkok to Chang Mai' on the side in big letters. The platform from which it was leaving was registered on both our tickets. We stowed our luggage, sat in our seats and were delighted to be served curry from a man who had a portable paraffin stove set up in the linked bit between the next carriage and ours. We had especially opted for no air conditioning, because we like the climate of Thailand and don't like to freeze.

The train pulled out at precisely 6 pm.

Once out in the countryside we would stop only at the odd station, but on the edge of Bangkok there were a number of suburban halts where people could board. At about 7 pm a Thai family entered our carriage. There was dad, mum and two children. The man looked at us, looked at his tickets, and said, 'Madam and sir, you are in our seats.'

I took out my own tickets, looked at the seat numbers, checked the carriage number, and shook my head.

'You've made a mistake. These are our seats.'

He shrugged and showed me his tickets. I showed him mine. They were identical. Damn railway clerks, I thought. They've either sold the seats twice, or made a stupid error. All those ledgers too! You would think the system infallible with so much bureaucracy.

'I must fetch the ticket inspector,' said the Thai gentleman. 'He'll know what to do.'

'Good idea,' I replied, safe in the knowledge that possession was nine tenths of the law. 'He'll sort it out.'

In the meantime I offered my seat to the man's wife and Annette chatted to the two children.

The ticket inspector turned out to be a corpulent official covered in gold lanyards, medals and scrambled egg. He looked like an amiable general in Thailand's army. However, he was accompanied by a lean narrow-eyed lieutenant who wore a gun at his hip. This one looked like an officer in the Vietcong, the one from the movie 'The Deerhunter' who keeps yelling, '*Wai! Wai! Wai!*' or some such word into the ear of Robert de Niro. This man's hand never left his gun butt as he stared at me from beneath the slanted peak of his immaculate cap.

Neither of these rail officials spoke English.

The ticket inspector studied all the tickets on show and then spoke softly to the gentleman with the nice family.

'He wants to know,' said the gentleman, turning to me, 'why you are on the wrong train?'

We were nonplussed. Stunned. Gobsmacked.

'What wrong train?' I argued. 'This is the 6 pm from Bangkok to Chang Mai, isn't it?'

'No,' came the calm reply, 'this is the 3 pm from Bangkok to Chang Mai, running late as usual.'

'What? You mean . . .'

'All trains run late here, sir. The 6 pm will still be standing in the station. The ticket inspector says you will have to get off at the next station and wait for your right train.'

Annette and I stared out of the window at the blackness rushing by. The country stations had no lights whatsoever. They were pits of darkness in a world of utter darkness. I had visions of standing on one of those rickety wooden platforms trying to flag down an express. It was scary. Too scary to contemplate. I'm sure the people who lived near those stations were perfectly respectable citizens, but the night time jungle does things with the imagination. There was no way we were going to get off our train, now that we were rattling towards Chang Mai.

Through our gentleman translator we managed to persuade the inspector to let us stay on the train. At first he wanted to sell us first class tickets to the air conditioned compartments. When that didn't work - Annette digging in her heels - he found us similar seats to the ones we already had. It occurred to me he could have done that in the first place, but since all was well that ended well, I really didn't care.

There is a post script to this short tale.

To avoid any repetition of this near horror story, we chose to return to Bangkok by a reliable bus. I kid you not when I say that when we boarded the coach our pre-booked seats were completely overflowing with Thai monks. We explained to these orange-robed young men that they were in our seats and they pointedly ignored us, staring out of the window. I fetched the driver who said, 'Sir, as monks they are permitted to sit anywhere, eat anything, and the law tells us we can do nothing.' Since young men serve a year or two as monks, in the way that they do their national service in the army, we weren't too impressed by the piety side of things. They were not dedicated holy men, having taken vows of poverty, but ordinary youths serving out a set time.

The guys wouldn't budge. They knew their rights.

A fierce woman conductor told us to 'get off the bus'. We told her we had tickets for the seats these two queue jumpers were sitting in. We were not going to move. Other passengers began to get restless. The driver started looking panicky. Finally he came to us with his hands clasped as if in prayer and said, 'Sir, Madam, I beseech you. I plead with you to understand my problem and leave the bus.' We sighed, gave up and got off the vehicle. It's a tough man who can withstand a Thai beseeching, I can tell you. Tougher than me, anyway. We collected our luggage from underneath the bus and waited for the next one. Hopefully the place had run out of monks and we could get back to Bangkok. And where do Thai bus drivers learn words like 'beseech'? I guarantee half the population of the English-speaking world doesn't know that word. He probably had a degree in English Literature, having read Chaucer and *Piers Ploughman*, while all I know of Thai is 'good day'.

One problem began to mar my voyage through the Outback. Although I had managed to phone Annette at Gayndah on the first evening, I hadn't managed to contact her since then. She had taken the tilt train from Brisbane to Cairns, then set out for some Quaker Friends located on the Atherton Tablelands.

The trouble was we both had UK mobiles which for some reason would not work in the Outback. I borrowed Pete's Aussie mobile but by that time Annette had disappeared into the Tablelands, a remote area of rainforest and bush, where she would be looking for wildlife. (She eventually became 'the platypus lady' having located some of these strange creatures and asked by the eco lodge to take out parties to see them). Her location was as bad as mine, for cell phone reception. I knew she would be worrying about how I was managing, but I couldn't get hold of her. (In fact, we would not manage to speak again until I reached Innot Springs near the end of the ride, though she had by that time contacted one of the organisers' mothers and ascertained I was not in surgery).

It would have been nice to get all excited by each day's events and share them with Annette on the going down of the sun, but hey, when we were first married the Royal Air Force sent me to South Yemen for a year during which we could only communicate by letter, and it had been far more dangerous then, since I was being shot at, probably quite rightly, by anti-colonialist Arabians who wanted me out of their country almost as much I wanted to get out.

DAY FOUR

Brolga cranes, wedge-tailed eagles and whistling kites seemed to litter the sky on the morning of the fourth day of our Outback challenge. Dan had said more than once that he preferred 'challenge' to either 'adventure' or 'rally'. Indeed, it was a challenge. The bikes were small and the roads were beginning to get rougher.

Before I left UK I'd shown someone a picture of the Honda 110 and he sneered and called it a 'girlie bike'. Well hell, mate, it's a lot more difficult ploughing through dirt on a girlie bike than on a 650 Macho Machine like Charlie and Ian use. The narrow tyres, the lack of engine power, the weight of the goods on the rear, all make the little Honda difficult to handle off road.. It dances on the dust. It would pirouette if it was allowed to. It certainly bucks like an ornery mule at odd times, just when you're not expecting it. No worries, mate, the Postie Bike's no girlie when it comes to battling with cracks and craters. I said to the critic, 'What would be easier, pal – crossing the Atlantic on a cruise ship or setting off in a girlie rowboat?'

I knew from Pete we were coming to bull dust days and keeping one's bum on the seat was not going to be as easy as before. But I just loved the scenery in the mornings. The sense of foreverness did not go away. In fact it increased. I recalled the lines from a poem by the American, Robert Frost: 'You cannot scare me with your spaces between the stars, where no human race is, I have it in me much nearer home, to scare myself with my own desert places'. Of course, he could have been talking about the empty places in our lives or in our spirits –

poets are deep fellahs when you start to probe – but equally he may have meant the Australian Outback.

As I hummed along the empty highway, heading out into the sandy-coloured unknown, I thought about the previous night's camp at Barcaldine. We camped at the show ground where there just happened to be a country show in progress. Tractors there were in plenty, and rare breed sheep, cattle, horses, tame carpet snakes, quad bikes, pies, beer, and all the rest of the paraphernalia you find at country fairs everywhere. All the men wore big cowboy hats and all the women sported big cowgirl hats. There was line dancing in a cowshed and Country songs belting out from a barn. We were no longer the main curiosity, us postie bike riders. There were other serious contenders for that crown at Barcaldine.

Most of our riders put up their tents in an empty cattle stall or stable. I preferred the open air. It didn't seem right putting up a tent without using the pegs.

The Country songs went on until the early hours of the morning, but I was so tired from the long haul along the bitumen, with its 'white-line fever', that I just fell onto my air bed and went out like a light.

Again, today, it's all bitumen, or bitch-u-men, as some of the riders called it. I love the Aussie habit of twisting the words to get something quite outrageously descriptive from it.

At noon I passed a rider with a blown front tyre.

As always, we crossed over several dry creeks, all of them with original names, some of them quite intriguing. 'Big Dinner Creek' and later, 'Little Dinner Creek'. One creek we crossed must have brought a smile to everyone's face. It was called 'Christmas Creek' and it was way out in the bush, 2000 kms from anywhere, not a house in sight, not a town for miles, yet someone had decorated its stunted trees with tinsel, baubles and paperchains.

How's that for an Aussie sense of humour?

It's as quirky as the British.

Near where I live in the UK is a town called Great Dunmow where every year since the Middle Ages they have held the Dunmow Flitch Trials. This 'court' awards a 'flitch' (a side of bacon) to married couples from anywhere in the world if they can satisfy the a jury of 6 maidens and 6 bachelors that they have been married for a least 'twelvemonth and a day' and have not during that time wished themselves unmarried. There are many such idiosyncracies in many odd towns in the UK.

Australia has invented its own such bizarre events. One of the more famous ones takes place in Alice Springs every year and is called the Henley-on-Todd regatta. The Todd River is dry baked earth. Every spring 'No Fishing' signs go up along the dusty banks of this Aussie wadi and people start building boats with holes in the bottom. The contestants stick their legs through the holes and race the boats along the hot sandy bottom of a waterless river bed. There are 'yachts', 'Oxford tubs', and bottomless 'eights'. Those taking part are bombarded with flour bombs and other such weapons. The town is 1,500 kms from the nearest body of water. Some of those taking part are said to be sane.

Later that day, I was on my own, travelling through the eerie landscape of Dreamtime, when out of the dust haze came a shimmering line of dark riders on even darker Harleys. Black bandannas swathed their faces, black sunnies covered their eyes, black beards wrapped their chins, black dome-helmets sat uneasily on their heads - black everything, everywhere.

Sinister. Strange. Weird.

I felt a tingling go through me. They could have been phantom riders from 'Lord of the Rings', except they were on big bikes, not horses. They passed me by with barely a flicker of acknowledgement, me on my little red pony and they on their big black war horses. I stopped a little later and took a drink and mused for a while. I got to wondering if they were the Christmas Creek Chapter of the Hell's Angels, on their annual pilgrimage to decorate their shrine.

Afterwards I learned they were members of Bikers United Against Child Abuse. Good blokes, not bad guys.

Anyway, today it was Barcaldine to Winton, a journey of 294 kms, making our total mileage – sorry, kilometreage – to date 1554 kms. Had we ridden so far, so quickly? Who was I to doubt the speedo? 294 kms was an easy ride, especially on tarmac, so we had time to dawdle and gape. We would be passing through Longreach, where stood the Stockman's Hall of Fame and the QANTAS Museum. I had seen stockmen out in the fields, riding their stock horses. Grizzled, sunburnt, star-burnt faces, some of them Aboriginal. Hard, tough-looking characters that one associates with Australia. Never mind your mid-Western USA cowboys, these stockmen were as granite and teak fused together. They looked a part of the landscape over which they rode.

'Are we stopping at the Hall and Museum?' I yell to Pete and John, as we pause to water the bush.

Pete says, 'Don't worry about Quaint-arse, but you might find the Hall of Fame quite interesting.'

And so we did. It was indeed an interesting museum, full of tack and tackle, and farm machines, and pictures and stories of famous Outback men. You have to be someone special to live and die in the Outback. It must be a hell of a lonely life, but probably a fulfilling one. They know who they are. Us city folk (OK, I live in a Suffolk village, but I have travelled the world) really never find out who we are. They have their daily tasks and they get down and do them and don't whinge or whine or sweat over their lot in life.

I felt the same about the gold miners of the Canadian Yukon, when I visited Dawson City, that clapboard town on the Klondike where bitumen is unknown. Many hope-filled miners still exist there. They eke out a living from their mines these days, not striking it rich, but finding enough nuggets to make ends meet, so that they can continue to look for more nuggets. They're called 'sour doughs' in Canada, after the sour bread dough they used to take with them to last out the terrible -50 degree winters you get in the Yukon.

You have to know who you are to be digging in the ground in weather like that, not even guaranteed enough gold to make a decent tooth filling.

I learned at the Hall of Fame that the Aussie stock horse is possibly the most versatile horse in the world. It's known as, 'The breed for every need'. Tough, resilient and strong, they have the speed of a cheetah and the agility of a mountain goat. (In fact they reminded me of our Honda postie bikes.) Among other things, such as polo and show jumping, the stock horse is apparently good at campdrafting. I have to admit at that point in time I had no idea what 'campdrafting' was.

The Australian stock horse grew out of a one-time need for military mounts and work horses that were required for a variety of army tasks over the last two centuries. This led to the all-rounder we know today as the Aussie stock horse. I also heard these beasts referred to as 'walers' but whether that strictly meant horses from New South Wales or not, I failed to discover. Today you can buy a three-year old second-hand Honda 110 for about $1000, whereas a stock horse will set you back at least $3000, but more likely $10,000. If you feel you need one, go to Dalby Queensland in December of any year, but if you want a *really* good goer in a private sale, take along a thick wad of notes amounting to somewhere in the region of $200,000.

Back on the road I was passed by DIPSTICK BRO and GERONIMO, the road names written on the backs of two riders. I knew the latter was my pal from Leicestershire, John, but with a lot of the blokes and bloke-esses I never ever did get to know all the real names, so Dipstick remains Dipstick. We were heading now for Winton, home of Waltzing Matilda, the song written by Banjo Patterson. This was where he first performed the unofficial National Anthem of our antipodean cousins. It's a great song, once heard it buries itself in the psyche whether you are Australian or not, and is sadly mutilated by the Barmy Army when they're trying to get the under the skins of the Aussie team cricket supporters, bless their English socks.

Around mid-afternoon I was almost shouldered into a ravine by a road train. Road trains are truly terrifying creatures: the Tyrannosaurus Rex of the Outback. A monstrous cab pulling up to three long trucks taking up almost all the road space. This oblong giant appeared out of the heat haze on the highway enveloped in a huge cloud of dust which he kindly shared with every other road user, including me. I slowed down to pull of the track, as I was supposed to do, when I realised there was a drop off the edge about a metre deep. I had nowhere to go as the monster drew up alongside me, all 54 metres of him. He was a cattle truck and as well as dust there was the stink of penned animals to contend with. I was coughing and spluttering as he thundered past me with centimetres to spare, when from the other direction along comes another beast of the same magnitude. My truck then edges towards me to give the guy room on the other side of the road. Now I was riding on a strip of track only a few inches wide with the drop on my left yawning. I braked, not realising one of the other riders was right on my back wheel. He skidded up alongside me and we both teetered on the brink of oblivion for a few moments, before finally the road train squeezed away again.

Cold sweat mingled with the warm stuff, as I gathered myself together and tried to stop my heart from jumping out of my mouth. The other rider gave me a look. I gave him a look back. Then we both disentangled ourselves and sped away. I never did learn who he or she was: when you're all kitted up in your road armour you're virtually anonymous - but I never braked after that without looking in my rear view mirror, even if I did have the king of dinosaurs fighting me for road space.

We rolled into Winton in small groups, twos and ones like old-time sundowners, ready for the evening meal. It had been another day of mystical scenery and wide wide landscapes. Who would not be a sundowner or a swagman in this great country? It was made for the wanderer, the traveller through ancient ways. Hence, of course, the Walkabout, which had probably been going on since Man first arrived on the Australian shore in their little boats, looked around him, and said to his companion, 'Bloody hell, mate, we've picked a winner here. Never mind the weekend camping, we can do it all the time. The camping grounds go on forever.'

In those days, of course, he had to contend with prehistoric mammals such as the Doom Duck, a monstrous flightless bird that could swallow a pig whole, and various other big fellahs: marsupial lions, marsupial wolves and a load of huge lumpy looking monsters that might have been rhinos or hippos. No doubt the boys and girls slept in the forks of trees and never went Walkabout without a spear. It's not difficult even now to imagine those old mammals lumbering about the landscape, looking for new meat on two legs.

Our camp that night was in the local footy oval, where they play – well, *play* is a sort of loose word when it comes to Aussie rules football, since the object seems to be to murder as many of the opposing players as possible – that unfathomable blood sport which only Australians understand, but many other nationalities enjoy watching in the way that they would the spectacle of gladiators killing each other in an arena.

The area was already littered with tents that were up, tents that were half up and tents that were flat as pancakes. Riders were milling about, talking, drinking beer, getting showers, doing bike maintenance. It was the gathering of the herd. Stories were being swapped. Disasters were being recounted. So-and-so had gone into a ditch and bent his gear lever. Whatisname had blown a tyre and had ended up in a thorn tree. Thingymejig had run out of gas out in the plains of nowhere and couldn't start his bike for twenty minutes after refuelling. Such conversations floated through the evening ether as the herd milled.

Once the tents were up and showers taken we were conveyed in a bus to a kind of craggy hill top similar to the one in the movie *Picnic at Hanging Rock*. It appeared to be an ancient place, no doubt with

Dreamtime significance. There were gullies and strangely-shaped rocks sculpted by wind and water out of the landscape. It did not take much to imagine carpet-snake-people and hare-wallaby-people meeting here to foment war or seal a peace. The view over the plains was awesome. A sort of scarred browny-red landscape stretched out on all sides, mile upon mile upon mile, to the far horizons.

We watched as the sun went down behind a distant range of hills and I'm sure we all experienced that humble feeling one gets while witnessing a natural occurrence where a fantastic but simple beauty is produced by a common-or-garden event – simply, the end of an ordinary day. The rays of the dying sun stretched out over the russet landscape to enhance the ochre redness of the soil. It could have been the end of a Jurassic day, or as it actually was, a day several million years after giant lizards lumbered over the land. Certainly the ghosts of dinosaurs were there, tramping over that ancient earth.

Once the natural phenomenon of a huge dark-red sun sinking into a vast dark-red landscape had ended and things spiritual gave way to things mundane, we tucked into a great meal provided by the Winton Lions Club. The yarns began, the camaraderie growing with every day. Any wariness had now been tucked away as riders got to know each other better and like-minded people swapped biking tales, stories of where they came from and what they did, and all those exchanges that happen when a group starts coming together.

Over these exchanges I learned that Ewan, my new buddy from Darwin, had had to change his bike for one of the spares. His first bike refused to start after he'd stopped at the Stockman's Hall of Fame. I stroked my own machine, hoping she would not prove as fickle. So far she had been an absolute beauty, starting every time, running as smoothly as a young filly. I did have one bit of trouble, but that was my fault. I found out that if I turned off the engine while it was still in gear I had hell's own job of getting it into neutral. It *had* to go into neutral, because you couldn't start it in gear. If you did it would leap out of your hands like a kangaroo with its pants on fire and bury itself in the nearest inanimate object.

I kicked down and kicked down, but realised I would do some damage if I jumped on the gear lever any harder. So cap in hand I went to Richard-the-mechanic, who showed me how to gently rock the beast back and forth until she slipped into neutral. From that moment on I never switched off the engine while the bike was in gear. I thanked Richard humbly – thanks he waved away with a yeah-sure – aware that my biker inexperience had shown, probably not for the first time.

'What did you think of the Hall?' asked Ewan, over a beer.

'Not a bad little museum,' I said. 'How about you? You're a local. Did you learn anything?'

'Probably, but what struck me most were the items which displayed as being part of the pioneer's time – the early days of the bush. Things like saddler's repair kits, wind-up telephones and milk delivered in billy cans. What worries me is *I* remember those things as a kid. It makes me feel old.'

Ewan is about a quarter of a century my junior.

'Listen,' I said, 'I remember when eggs came as dried powder in cans – you ain't as old as me, mate. I was six years old before I saw a real egg and I thought it was a squashed tennis ball . . .' But though things were starting to get fanciful, I really had known a time when dried egg and powdered lemonade came to our house in cans, back in the olden days.

There were stories about the road kills we had seen that day – feral pigs, kangaroos of course, even cattle. Ewan also told the tale of the live black snake that was minding its own business, crossing the road, when a line of riders came at it. The first rider tried to miss the creature, but this local serpent was stretched from one side of the bitumen to the other. In the event, the lead postie biker clipped its tail. The snake was naturally incensed at this uncalled-for treatment and reared up, swishing itself about as other riders come upon it. There was a great deal of dodging and swerving, as bikers fought to remain upright without hitting the snake or getting bitten.

'The choreography was brilliant,' said a tall Irish-Australian, a three-timer on the Postie Bike Challenge. 'Nureyev could not have done it better.'

Oh, and one of the guys told me what 'campdrafting' is. It's sort of herding cattle in a precise way. The stockman cuts out one of the herd and hustles it into a pen the way a Welsh Border Collie does with a sheep. Something like that. Apparently it's become a popular rodeo sport with youngsters and oldsters proving their skill with the stock horse. Good Outbacky stuff.

DAY FIVE

RUNNING SHEET
2008 Brisbane - Cairns
via the Gulf

The following running sheet has been provided as a guide only.

Day 5 continued		
105.1	487	Straight on past Norollah off to left
		Cross two causeways
123.6	516	Take fork to LEFT. CAUTION! Most traffic appears to go right
145.2	537	Windmill and grid
152.1	544	Straight on past Glenlyon off to left
166.1	558	Right at T-intersection
176.6	568	Turn hard Left to WOLSTON/COLLERAINE MaMaxweton)
177.1	568.5	As a check, you should cross a grid shortly with truck tyres.

78

179.4	571	Keep to Right- Past Colleraine homestead
199	591	Wollston off to right
207.7	599	Straight on past Wimmera/Winchester ccrossroads crossroad.
224.5	616	Right Turn
230.5	622	Left Turn to TARBRAX / JULIA Ck CkCREEK
231.7	624	Right Turn (veer right) to JULIA Ck CREEK
250.1	642	Straight on past Belford/Ardbrin cross road
260	652	Right turn at Junction (Helen Downs) off to left)
274	666	Edith Downs off to Left
280.2	672	Left Turn immediately over 2nd grid to PROA
285.1	677	Turn Left to PROA- about 4k in to homestead

TODAY'S F U E L STOP Corfield

The second column on the running sheet is the one we had to fill in ourselves, working forward from the kilometres on our speedos. There is no guarantee that my arithmatic is correct here. I do not have a head for maths and I probably filled it in by torchlight in the early dawn, while sitting with a bunch of noisy eaters at the breakfast table. This is the sheet we would attach to our handlebars in a plastic envelope, using sticky tape. It flapped around so hard in the slipstream it was impossible to read without holding it still with the left hand, while glancing up and down at the road. My running sheet nearly caused the death of me and would have caused the death of several kangaroos if they hadn't already been run over by monster trucks or four-wheel drives.

Climbing out of my tent at 5.30 am I looked up to see a marvellous cloud. They call it Morning Glory here in Queensland. It's a giant rolling wave of white cloud, like a tsunami crossing the sky. I've never seen any other cloud like it in my life. For serene beauty nothing surpasses it. For elegant, majestic motion, there is nothing more poetic. You just have to do what I did - gape at it in wonder. I wanted to climb up there into the heavens and lay in its path, let it wash over me.

My diary told me it was bull dust day. Here at last. No more talk. The real deal. Now, you novice, you green Pommy bastard, your lack of experience and biking skills will be tested to the limit. Oh you idiot, what the hell were you thinking of, biking across the Ozzie Outback with only six weeks on-road biking experience?'

I have never owned a bike. This postie bike was my first. All my 12 one-hour lessons had been on an Italian motor scooter, an automatic with wheels the size of jam jar lids. Riding that machine prepared me for nothing but a gentle chug along Felixstowe sea front. Sure, I had had four days my postie bike now, but very little of that had been on gravel or dirt. So, with about 40 hours flying time I was about to go solo. I recalled the hellish day I had spent with John on a dirt bike, ploughing through the thick mud of Essex and Hertfordshire in the rain. That was supposed to be training for something like this. Somehow a day in the wetlands, on a bike that was taller than a lamp post, wasn't going to help me much out here in the arid wastelands of Mad Max country.

I told Pete we would not be riding together.

'I'll only slow you and John up. You shoot off and leave me to my battles with the shires of Queensland.'

Pete tells me, 'Head up, look ahead, keep the revs up when you hit the soft stuff. If the bike starts to lose it's rear end, drop down a gear and plough through it. Don't grip the handlebars too tight, stand on the pegs if you need a bit of central weight. You'll be okay.'

The destination was Proa Station, a once sheep farm out in the middle of nowhere. We went out in our usual manner, with the young blades shooting off in front, the older riders not greatly worried about coming in first, second or third, and finally a big bunch whose individuals keep changing places when they get fed up of being near or at the back. On this day I was somewhere in the middle, but would end up about two thirds down the pack when Proa came into view.

Clown-suited Scotty, Cam and Murray, three larakins but good riders, were as usual way out in front. Scotty had been given a special cap by Dan for spending time helping others on the ride. I understood he was a rally driver as well as a biker and obviously had good mechanical skills. I was barely a competent operator of a machine, let alone a diagnostician or surgeon. I was still learning what things were called – (Er, cut-out switch?) - and although I'd drilled myself to do all the maintenance necessary, if something went wrong inside – like if a thingy got jammed in a thingy – I was stumped. Scotty was a guy you could call on in such emergencies – if you could catch the bloke.

We refuelled at Corfield outside a pub and my running sheet told me to look for RICHMOND-SESBANIA after that, apparently written on a big truck tyre. We then went onto the dirt.

At first I was surprised by the track. It didn't seem too bad. We had already ridden on hard-surface dirt, with rocks and stones embedded, which was where we lost Jack. On that surface I managed to keep my speed up in the seventies. Today I was more cautious, keeping it down in the sixties, but mostly because of the horror stories I'd been fed. Soon I began to get a bit arrogant. This is easy, I thought. What the hell were we worried about? Even a sign that said, 'TRAFFIC HAZARD AHEAD – WHEEL RUTS, BULL DUST AND CORRUGATED SECTIONS – DRIVE WITH EXTREME CARE' did not faze me at all. I was cutting a swathe over this red dust without a care in the world.

I stopped for a drink at one point and Lang pulled up in a truck alongside.

'You all right?'

'Yeah,' I said, and going all Aussie, 'no worries.'

'Better than last year,' he indicated, nodding at the track. 'The bull dust has all but disappeared from this section.'

'Oh really,' I replied, thinking, thank God for that.

'Yes,' he said, 'but there'll be some later on, you can bet on that.'

Oh, great, I thought.

A road train went past us both. 54 metres of it. Three articulated waggons. It covered us in a cloud of dust which didn't settle for about five minutes. As I've already said, road trains are the biggest and most dangerous hazard of the Outback. These huge trucks got up quite a speed and you have to get off the road if you see one coming. They can't stop suddenly without jack-knifing, so anything in their way just gets mown down. They carry cattle, goods, fluids. They're monsters. Giants of road and track. Luckily you can see them coming from miles away by the dust cloud they leave in their wake.

This one was going in the same direction as me, but when they come towards you their slipstream is like a solid wall of air. It can knock you out of the saddle. I was always a bit wobbly on my wheels. One minute I would be doing 70 kms, then a passing road train slipstream would instantly brake me down to 30.

Scary things, road trains. They will henceforth haunt my nightmares. I wonder Steven Spielberg hasn't made a horror movie of a road train – oh, wait a minute, what about 'Duel'? That was one of his first movies, wasn't it? Well believe me, the sinister black truck in 'Duel' is a baby next to those monsters, the road trains.

I got back on my bike, toed her up into third gear, and set off once again on the powdery surface. We had about 200 kms of track to cover to Proa Station and I'd done a good stretch of it. I was feeling quite merry. Then a real motorcycle came out of the billowing dust and haze and waved me down. The bloke removed his helmet and bid me a very good day, sitting astride this wonderful BMW, 650 I think, but it could have been more. If his bike had fallen over as bikes sometimes do, I wouldn't have the strength to get it upright again. It was huge and the throaty engine growled contentedly like a male lion after a mating session.

'Nice bike,' I said, wondering if I should have called it a hog, or something street-talky like that. 'Must go over the ruts easier than this one.'

'Yeah – but, hey look, watch out a bit further on – the road gets worse the nearer you get to Proa. Good luck.'

Sure enough, the dust began to thicken under the tyres. *Now* we were in bull dust country. The bike began to slither and slide away from under me every few yards. My speed got slower and slower, until I was doing 30-40 kms, sometimes less when the ruts threw me into the central bull dust pile, or out on the edge where the build-up was just as bad. Sometimes it was six inches to a foot deep in places and the back end of the bike was doing a dance all of its own, not paying any attention to my steering at all.

'Who's the master of this thing?' I yelled at the rear end. 'Me or you?'

It was definitely, *you*. A fly got in my helmet, the bridge of my nose was killing me where my glasses were digging in underneath the pressure of the goggles, and I was sweating and itching from every pore. I stopped for a moment and watched others. Some bikers were ice skating just like me, while others seemed to hold a dead straight line. It looked easy, as the good ones simply cruised past me, not going fast but doing a reasonable speed. They could have been delivering nitro-glycerine in their milk crates for all anyone would guess.

Envious of this skill I got back on and falling in behind one of the good guys, tried to emulate his riding. It did me no credit when my bike continued to swerve and skid. What was I doing wrong? Maybe the speed was too slow? I tried speeding up and nearly came a cropper. I slowed down again to about 30 kms. I felt it would be a shame to come off the bike so near to the station. Others had, I knew. I could see the skids of those who had gone before, with the occasional hollow mark where someone had taken a fall. So far my bum had stayed on the saddle, despite several near tumbles.

When I looked over my shoulder, down that long and dusty road, the heat haze warped the riders coming up behind me. The drifting clouds of dust mingled with the snaking ribbons of heat thrown up by the earth and created a kind of red-dust fog. Riders came out of it like dark phantoms rippling into view. Some of them were wobbling and skidding, others keeping a slow straight path, but all were shimmering, serpentine shapes that appeared as crinkled ghostly shadows and gradually formed into solid human beings on motorbikes. It was an eerie sight that held my attention for quite a while. As a writer of speculative fiction this scene was something right out of a fantasy story.

I shook my head clear and continued on my own unsweet way, ploughing through that same hot dust.

Here's one of the problems with being a rookie. The motor scooter on which I had learned my trade and passed my test, was an automatic. Since there's no clutch, automatics have both brakes on the handlebars. The left hand lever is the front brake, the right hand lever is the back brake. On semi-automatics, e.g. the Hondo postie bike, the right hand lever is the *front* brake, the rear brake being down by the right foot. So, where I had been trained to apply the back brake was now where the front brake was located. Thus, in moments of panic I grabbed the right hand lever mistakenly thinking I was applying the back brake. Once or twice this almost had me flying through the air, over the jolly old handlebars, and into the path of my own machine.

The last thirty kilometres were agony. Finally the driveway into the farm came into view. I tootled along this track and found John and Pete sitting in the sun gulping down beers. I felt a little triumphant, I had to admit. I certainly wasn't the last bike in by a long shot and I had stayed in the saddle. Pete congratulated me. So did John. It was all, all so premature. I thought Proa would be the worst day. It wasn't. The worst was yet to come. I would indeed part company with my beloved machine, several times, but for now I was happy.

However, both my hands ached from gripping the bars, even though Pete had given both John and me a little gadget – a sort of cruise control clip-on plastic spur – which required very little pressure to keep the revs up. I could not open my fingers for a while and walked about with hawk's talons. My shoulders, my back, and my neck also ached like mad. In fact the only part that didn't hurt, the part which I had expected to hurt, was my bottom. I had spent so much time up on the pegs, my backside had hardly touched the saddle that day.

Two people had to be medivaced. Anna, who had already hurt her ankle, damaged herself further on the ride to Proa and was whisked away from us by men in green.

Also one of the guys had dislocated his shoulder. He walked about for a while, bearing the pain stoically, but in the end had to give in to his fate and was out of the challenge.

Among the other guys thrown off that that day, was one a mechanic told us who was, ' . . . motionless, face down in the bull dust, slowly suffocating . . .' That treacherous red powder. It bucked you off your bike and then did its best to drown you.

A brave guy with a brave face. But you can't have a dislocation like that and carry on riding a motorcycle. The greenies took him off that evening.

Proa Station no longer seemed interested in sheep. There were a few emus about, and a nuisance of a gobbling male turkey who tried to flirt with everything that moved on two legs. I kept my legs out of the way. Dogs are always trying to hump my legs. I wanted no bloody Outback turkey trying it on, even with shin-guard protection.

Duncan, the owner, took us on a tour and explained what the sheep ranch did now.

'We farm red claw crayfish in ponds now,' he said, 'ponds fed by fresh water from down below, which comes up through a bore hole. The red claws grow to about 14 or 15 centimetres long and make a good meal.'

I can't remember how deep the artesian well was, but I remember being very impressed. When harvesting time comes they drain the ponds to about two-feet deep then set up a large vat in the middle. The vat is located up stream of the flow and the natural instinct of the crayfish is to walk against the current, perhaps to find the source. This leads them up a ramp and into the barrel, so to speak, harvesting themselves.

Over a drink Pete told me that the local fauna included the Green Tree Frog. Since this particular Ozzie frog is normally found in damp rainforest conditions, and the Outback at Proa is dry and dusty with hardly a tree to be seen, I found this a bit hard to believe and said so.

'Ah,' said Pete, supping his ale, 'you have to take into account flush toilets.'

It seems the Green Tree Frog has chosen another environment to live out his life cycle. This fellah is now found in cisterns all over the Outback and where the cisterns are of the overhead variety he makes his home in the ceramic bowl itself, gripping under the rim with tenacious feet when some thoughtless user flushes the toilet.

Duncan had a story of a Green Tree Frog which caused a disturbance in the shearers' quarters one night. The building had been cleaned up for some city visitors and Duncan had particularly checked the toilet for stray frogs before allowing his guests inside. Not well enough, apparently. A middle-aged woman went into the toilet but within seconds screamed and took the dunny door off its hinges in her rush to escape. When calmed she told how she had just sat down when 'something cold and slimy' leapt at her from within the bowl.

That evening we were fed by the Country Women's Association. Someone left in a light plane while we were eating, which seemed a good way to get out of the dust bowl we were in. The man with the big shiny BMW bike arrived back at the farm and stayed for the evening, before setting off in the dark – oh what fools these mortals be – back to someplace about sixty miles away. We had corned beef hash that night, which was wonderful cuisine. There was other fare, dishes too numerous to mention, including wonderful afters.

Lose weight? What a laugh! I have never eaten so well as on that ride, not in Hong Kong, not in London, not in any city restaurant or hotel anywhere. Ladies of the Outback, gentlemen of the Outback, I salute you - you are chefs extraordinary!

I put up my tent in the yard, along with John and Pete, while many others slept in the shearers' huts. That night the heavens were encrusted with stars. I never felt so good as I lay there on my airbed looking through the open flap at the trillions of bright chips of light embedded in the darkness. One of nature's great shows. And yes, the Southern Cross was still there. From the backyards of Oz they can see all five stars of the Southern Cross, and naturally that's how the constellation appears on the Australian flag. New Zealand also has the same constellation on its flag, but with only four of its stars since the Kiwis live around the corner of the world and are denied sight of the smaller fifth star.

The sixth star on the Australian flag, is the Federation star.

Since my trip people at home have asked me whether I was worried about snakes or spiders, with leaving the flap wide open all night. It never crossed my mind. Such creatures have never really bothered me. I was raised in Aden and camped in the Hadramaut Desert as a boy. I've lived in tropical lands most of my days. Snakes and spiders worry those who live in temperate lands. When you've been used to the wilderness on your doorstep, such creatures are commonplace. All right, I wouldn't want a coral snake or camel spider in my bed with me: they're both bloody poisonous bastards. But they don't want to be there either, so the feeling's mutual. I don't love 'em, but they don't worry me.

Earlier it had been another beautiful sundown which crept gently over the broad long plain. If I had lived in central Queensland all my life, I would probably belong to the Flat Earth Society. Much of it is as flat as paper, mostly dust, with the occasional pink grasslands. A spiritual land, without question, so no wonder its first inhabitants are a spiritual people with a deep belief in the mystical offerings of the landscape.

As I lay there that night, I got to thinking about the previous day's surreal experience with Christmas Creek and the black riders. I have had one or two 'surreal' happenings at Christmas, the weirdest being in Sumatra while I was waiting with Annette on the shores of a lake called Toba, in an area of volcanoes. It was Christmas day and we had walked down through the market to the water's edge, one of those markets where the locals spread blankets and sell a small pile of beans, nuts or fruit. One of those markets where you want to buy something from everyone, so they don't go home disappointed to their families.

We were just in the process of buying tickets for a ferry to an island on the lake when a four-wheel-drive vehicle skidded to a halt on the far side of the market. A Caucasian man got out dressed in a red suit trimmed with white, a black belt, big black boots, a false white beard, and a belly as big as a bass drum. He ran down to the edge of the shoreline and with arms akimbo, stared out over the waters of the lake. Then he let out an expletive, a nice rich juicy swearword in English, then marched back to his vehicle and drove off at high speed.

Not only were the market sellers agog, so were Annette and I, and also the ferry ticket seller. We all stood there with our eyes out on stalks. The event had been so abrupt and sudden it had knocked all the wind out of everyone's sails. Previous to this the only European faces we had seen was at local Methodist church when some tourists had gathered to sing carols with Christian Indonesians.

Then to cap the strangeness of the event, the ticket seller said with awe in his voice, 'Who was that? Moses?'

'No,' Annette replied, 'Santa Claus!'

For some inexplicable reason this knowledge caused the ticket seller to let out a sigh of disgust.

'Oh, *him*,' he said.

Who the ex-pat guy was, what he was doing in the middle of the Sumatran countryside dressed as Father Christmas, and why he was so angry, we never discovered. Nor did we find out why Moses was so revered and Santa Claus so despised by the Indonesian ticket seller. The whole scene took on a dream-like effect which faded into oblivion – until Christmas Creek reminded me of it, on the previous day's ride.

As with previous nights, someone at Proa was snoring very loudly. Several people, actually. It could have been the zoo, not a sheep station. We had been warned about this before coming on the challenge and I'd brought some earplugs with me. However, earplugs only work to a degree. They don't block out the noise completely. So I lay there sort of dozing and waking, the whole night, but feeling happy at having reached day five of the trip without injury.

DAY SIX

Someone told me at breakfast that we had actually lost a rider at Emerald. One of the blokes had damaged his back kick-starting the bike. It's easily done. A back can go just bending over and tying a shoelace. Poor devil, to have to leave the group after not even experiencing the high-flying excitement of going over the bars of his bike. That must have been a real bummer. I'd have been spitting bull dust.

A few of the lads found some skulls the previous day and had mounted them on their bike bars. These were the pure white headbones of dead rams, with beautiful curling horns, but they looked kind of sinister and cool as trophies on the front of the bikes. Big, bad riders and small mean-looking bikes. One rider had found a set of horns – ox by the look of them - and they too made a statement. The Wild Ones.

After a massive breakfast that would have fed an army, we gathered around Dan for the daily briefing. Today was another loooong ride. 459.5 kms. I was looking forward to the last .5 kms. I ached a bit from the previous day's battle with the bull dust. Perhaps it was my inexperience, gripping the bars too tightly, holding my body rigid instead of loosening up and going with the flow? Anyway, I was not looking forward to leaving Proa. We still had a few kilometres of dirt road and loose dust before we hit any solid ground. However, Dan told us the road out of Proa was better than the road in, so I thought to myself, 'Gotta learn to relax when I'm riding.'

We went out in our usual stream, 46 bikes now, all in a line, until the overtaking started and the wild ones went flying out in front, leaving their dust to be eaten. The headwinds were ferocious that day, forcing down the speed. Temperatures on the other hand, had risen, to around 35 degrees centigrade. There were kites and hawks feasting on kangaroo carcasses every few hundred metres. A bike passed me, with SQUIRTER written on the rider's back. And then TRYPOD, who was another Pom like myself. TRYPOD owned a good expensive camera and took some great photos with it, including some eagles and hawks which I'd specifically requested him to get for me. My own little camera was fine for most things, but photographing wildlife is an art and science in itself, and requires something more than a point and shoot.

YOU'VE BEEN PASSED BY ROGER was the next to throw dirt into my face with his back wheel. I said to Roger afterwards that a more penetrating statement on the back of his coat would have been YOU'VE JUST BEEN ROGERED, but alas they can't all be literary geniuses like moi. When I was thinking of writing something on my own back, I eventually put MONKEY CATCHER, the idea being 'Softly, softly catchee monkee', in that I would eventually finish the ride, no matter how slowly I went. In retrospect, I wish I'd put my other choice, which was MARVEST HOON, a spoonerism of HARVEST MOON. Australian 'hoons' being wild youths who drive bad boy cars at reckless speeds. However, this convolution seemed too erudite at the time.

I decided to ride alone again, given that we did have a good stretch of dirt road, and so let John and Pete shoot off. They were very competent riders, both of them, though John was ever impetuous and was known to leave the road and hurtle into paddocks to say hello to horses and other livestock. John is a wonderful talker and when he hasn't got anyone to listen, he probably talks to himself and his attention strays. There is nothing so cheery as John in the morning and he sort of bucks you up from the moment you rise. Good lad that he is.

However, our John is also fastidious. I'm amazed he was never a regular soldier in the army. I spent 18 years in the RAF and have some excuse for folding my shirts just so, but alongside John I'm a slob. Pete and I would stand waiting for John in the morning, as that man spent eons taking down his tent, packing his kit, and polishing the grass afterwards. Tent pegs would be lined up, poles standing to attention, clothes laid out just so. We all had to cram our gear in the army style kit bag – there was never enough room for tent, air bed, underwear, spare shirts, camping towel, air pump, and all the personal items – so even if stuff went in neatly, it came out looking like a jumble sale at the village hall.

Pete on the other hand is one of your taciturn Aussies. He would stand there watching John pack, shaking his head slowly and thoughtfully. Sometimes he growled. Sometimes he cast his eyes to heaven. We all have our foibles. I probably exasperated the pair of them, but heck, I'm lucky because I'm the one writing the book, and as far as I'm concerned, Kilworth is the perfect buddy to go on a bike ride with.

I got a bit of stick from John for not shaving and keeping the standard up – in Leicestershire they wear blazer and tie to the pub – but I did that anyway, later, because the bloody beard threatened to stifle me inside the helmet. It was one of those nightmarish imaginings, the hair growing and growing and filling the helmet until it finally suffocated the wearer. So I did shave, and I did wash out my underpants once or twice.

Underpants! Now there's an interesting subject for a bike riding challenge. Pete had warned me to get t-shirts and underpants that would dry quickly. You can get quick-drying clothes, towels, etc at any good camping shop. I'd got the towel and t-shirts, but not any underpants. Pete had also told me to bring boxer shorts, rather than briefs. I didn't know why and ignored the advice, bringing (it has to be said) mostly boxers, but two pairs of briefs also. I found out why.

On a bike you wear so much clobber you feel like a knight in armour. Once the stuff's on, you can't reach things like underpants without calling for your squire and having him assist you in de-armouring. I went out from Proa wearing briefs for the first time. Within two hours, having crossed the dreaded dust and found blessed tarmac again, I was writhing in agony. The briefs were cutting into the inside leg of my crotch like cheesewire. It was excruciating. I knew if I didn't stop soon I would sever both legs at the joints with the pelvis.

The motion of the bike – not the velocity but shaking and rattling – judders the rider forward all the time, while on the other hand for some inexplicable reason which has puzzled Greek philosophers from the beginning of time, underpant briefs remain static on the saddle. Rider shuffles forward, pants stay where they are. Pants then become a cutting instrument, trying to sever limb from torso.

I stopped to top up the fuel tank, but was exposed to girl bikers and cars going by every few minutes, so I couldn't strip and get rid of the offending item. There was no real cover off the highway. The bushes were pathetic little things that wouldn't have hidden a modest elf. The arboreal landscape was no better. The trees were stunted eucalypts – known affectionately as 'gum trees' in Oz – and acacias – known affectionately as 'wattles'.

Aussies, as you probably know, like to smooth awkward words – if they can't add an 'ie' to the end – sunnies, Pommies, etc – they give it a nickname. This has nothing to do with any lack of intellect. Aussies are at least as bright as any pommy bastard, most of them coming as they do from the same stock. It's more to do with liquidity of speech, having the words flow off the tongue. After all 'sunglasses' is not a word that poets instinctively find easy on the ear. 'Sunnies' is much more fluid. Americans call them 'shades' but they go for drama, rather than smoothness of speech.

I got back on my bike and rode on. Within the next hour there were genuine tears in my eyes. I became convinced that the Gestapo must have made their captives wear briefs, forcing them to ride small motorbikes until they burst into tears and spilled everything they knew about troop movements.

By lunch time I was desperate. The fuel stop for the day was a patch of stunted gum trees and wattles. Bugger, I thought. Not even an old oil drum to hide my white British bum. Then I had an idea. In with my compass and map (insurance against getting lost in the bush, like some tourists and even locals, who get out of their car for a toilet stop and end up lost and walkabouting until they die of thirst) I had a Swiss army knife. I got this weapon, reached down inside my rider's trousers and pulled up the edge of my briefs.

I slashed through one flank of the offending undies, then the other, and with great relief pulled the buggers out and threw them into a waste bin. Job done. Then I looked up to see I was being observed, with amusement, by one of the Aussie women riders. I grinned and shrugged. She laughed and turned away, and I saw WIND on her back.

I supposed she rode like the wind.

Going commando for the rest of the day was like having six birthdays all at once. I couldn't have been happier. The relief from pain was tremendous.

Regarding my map and compass. These were security blankets. I'm sure if someone gets lost out there, where there is nothing but empty red space, it's better staying where you are and waiting for help. As mentioned earlier, in my more anxiety-ridden moments I'd thought about bringing a GPS, but the expense did not justify the purchase. How much is your life worth, I asked myself before leaving England? Well, at least the cost of a compass, but a GPS? Not that much mate.

Two young bushmen who didn't get lost were Duncan and Donald McIntyre, mere youths at the time, who founded the town of Julie Creek in 1862. They named the town after their aunt after travelling from the south with 10,000 sheep and twenty-five horses. It's flat country around Julia Creek, once good cattle and sheep land, but now silver, lead and zinc mining has taken over. The area boasts a local marsupial which I did not see hair or pouch of, perhaps because it's nocturnal. It's called the dunnart. I would have liked to have seen a dunnart, simply because I'd never heard of the creature before passing Julia Creek. Also around the region somewhere is the Combo Waterhole, the billabong in *Waltzing Matilda,* but I didn't see that either. They've had fire, flood and drought in Julia Creek, and I wouldn't want to be there in mid-summer, that's for sure, because the temperatures climb to the forties.

I caught up with Pete and John at Julia Creek, joining them for coffee at the local cafe. Pete always likes a double-shot long black which takes the roof off your mouth. I don't like flat white (a sort of latte) but I like my coffee a bit less system-shocking than double-shot long blacks. In Spain I usually order an 'Americano with milk on the side', so I can mix my own brew and get the strength to my liking. I tried to do that in Oz, got into all sorts of muddles, gave up and joined Pete.

'Did you see the road sign about planes landing?' I asked.

John said, 'You mean the one that said, ROAD MAY BE USED AS AN EMERGENCY RUNWAY?'

'That's the beggar. I kept looking over my shoulder for Jumbo jets.'

'Hercules,' muttered Pete. 'Not Jumbos.'

'Well they're big enough to knock me off my bike,' I argued, having flown in many a Charlie 130 in my time in the RAF. 'Hercules aircraft are no microlights.'

'True.'

One of the lads, Cam, told us the clutch was slipping on his bike. My 21 still purred along, or rather screeched along, without a sign of a problem. I felt very privileged to own her. I loved her as I love my own children. It troubled me that at the end of the ride I would have to sell her into slavery.

After Julia Creek I headed for our destination for the night, which was a pub at Gregory Downs. I'd been told there was a river there, running past the pub, where we could all have a lark about and a swim. I'd not done any scallywagging up until then and was looking forward to it. The Gulf of Savannah seemed like a good place for larking around. The river at this point was supposed to be quiet tranquil water. I also thought to look out for the unique and spectacular Livistonia palm tree, but I must have missed it, both going in and coming out.

On the way to Gregory Downs we passed thousands upon thousands of termite mounds, like traffic cones covering a vast area. It was an amazing sight for a Pom, though the locals were not that impressed, having seen as much many times before I suppose. At a ten-minute stop later on, I spoke with a retired couple driving an RV, or campervan. There are hundreds of them in Oz where they're known as Grey Nomads. This pair were heading for the camp at Gregory. I was feeling frivolous and pretended I didn't know about the mounds.

'All these grave markers,' I said, 'there must have been quite a massacre here at some time.'

The man frowned. 'Termites,' he said.

'No,' said I, 'that can't be. Termites are little creatures, like ants. You wouldn't have big grave markers like that for termites.'

He closed one eye and I think he would have thumped me if I hadn't got on my bike and shot off down the road.

On the subject of termite mounds, we had a lass with us, Josie from the Sunshine Coast I believe. A schoolteacher. Josie decided to ride by one of the mounds and kick it, presumably to watch it disintegrate into dust particles. There were two big guys who watched out for others a lot of the time – I believe they too gained helper caps - but they failed to keep Josie out of trouble on this occasion. Josie found that termite mounds are as hard as concrete and she broke some toes. One more for the doctor at the next available clinic.

Gregory Downs pub was pretty good. There was vegetation down by the Gregory River. There were birds and signs of other wildlife. I liked the place. I tried to reach Annette again, but still no signal on my mobile. Pete's mobile worked fine, but it seemed that Annette's phone was still not in a state to receive the call. I knew she would be upset by this, but there was little I could do.

Since I wasn't going to use the bike again that day I decided to fill out my Running Sheet for the following morning. This was a horrible mental exercise for someone like me. I've never been great at arithmatic. In fact I'm crap. I'd got it wrong once or twice and had to use the rubber and start again. It was agony having to do it once, let alone twice over, so I furrowed my brow in concentration and used a piece of scrap paper to write down my calculations.

Gregory Downs to Normanton, past Burketown and over the Leichhardt River. My speedo read 38, 136 kms at this point in the journey. I added 93 kms to this figure which was the first stretch in the morning, making 38, 229 kms. When my speedo registered that figure I would have to **Right turn to BURKETOWN** according to my sheet. The next stretch was 119 kms, which again I added to the original 38,136 kms (*not* to the running total 38,229 as I had done once at the beginning of the ride, an exercise which would eventually result in a journey to the moon and back) making 38,255 before I had to right turn right again, to Normanton. Then the next stop, 190 kms further on, was the Leichhardt River, an historic crossing point, where we would refuel.

And so on, a whole sheet of figures which I taped to the bars of my bike each day. When I wanted to read this sheet, which was extremely difficult since with my glasses on my eyesight is remarkably poor at a distance of two feet, I would have to hold the shuddering, flapping sheet still with my left hand, squint down, glance up at the road, squint down, glance up, squint down, glance up – this series going on long enough for me to eventually read where I'm supposed to be going without leaving the road and hurtling into the bush.

Only twice on the whole ride did I take the wrong turning and somehow I instinctively knew I'd gone wrong, backtracked, waited for one of the others to come along. When I saw a red bike and had made sure it wasn't the local postie trying to fool me, I then took the same direction. Only twice, which I felt wasn't bad for a stranger in a strange land, and a rookie biker at that.

At the end of the day we would have done 341.9 kms and would hopefully be in the rodeo grounds of Normanton. Always the last 50 kms of the day were difficult for me, and I believe for others. I had to force my eyes to stay open. My bones and muscles ached with the juddering. My brain was full of bees. The bike engine seemed to get noisier and noisier, the mind and spirit got tired, and all I wanted to do was get to the end of the road. Some of the riders wore ear plugs and some carried ipods to drown out the grinding bike engine with pleasant music. If I'd thought to bring music of some kind I'd have gone for good Aussie folk.

Pete had introduced me to the *Bushwackers*, whose single favourite of mine is *Limejuice Tub*. The *Bushwackers*, now defunct, sing a great mix of Irish, English and plain old Aussie folk songs. If not the *Bushwackers*, then *Midnight Oil*, my favourite cd of theirs being *Diesel and Dust*. How appropriate would that be?

DAY SEVEN

And so, another day dawned over the vast hinterland of north-eastern Australia. Kookaburras, those charming sweet-voiced birds of the Queensland bush and billabong, woke me with their trilling. Their song can only be compared to the nightingale, for its musical range and depth of passion. Ha!

I rose – it was still dark of course – with my miner's light wrapped around my head. Packed my kit, washed and did certain other unmentionables in the ablutions, and then went to breakfast with my pals, Pete and John.

As usual at breakfast I read the Queensland edition of Lonely Planet and looked up the towns we were going through. I'm a huge fan of Tony Wheeler's Lonely Planet and have been since its conception. I bought one of the first copies of *Asia on a Shoestring*, and travelled the Far East with it back in the days when Tony Wheeler was a struggling entrepreneur and I was a young buck of just 50 years of age. Since that time he has published only one fiction book with his publishing company, an anthology of science fiction stories entitled *Not The Only Planet* which featured one of my own stories, the first I ever wrote, called *Let's Go To Golgotha*.

Today was Gregory Downs to Normanton. Burketown was on the way. I had thought Proa Station was going to be the most difficult ride. Wrong. Today was going to be the ultimate test of my basic biking skills (virtually zero), my stamina (pretty good), my spirit level (reasonably high) and my ability to bounce (which has got worse with age). However, there was some bitumen at first, and Burketown was an early stop.

Most of the bikes were behaving very well, with one or two exceptions. Murray Nettheim's little gem apparently changed gear of its own accord when he hit soft sand. Pete's bike was running too rich at one point and I think Scotty fixed that for him at a fuel stop. The engine of another lad's bike cut out at odd times leaving him coasting.

Murray's strange gear-changing sounded very frustrating, since he said it often jumped from 4th to 2nd without warning. Such a sudden change might have the rider somersaulting over the handlebars if he's not ready for it. Murray suggested that the bike had decided it was an automatic, rather than a semi. Or maybe the machine had decided it could read the road better than its rider? Who knows, one day perhaps Steven King will write a horror novel about it and there'll be a movie.

I always started 21 after breakfast, ran her for a few minutes to warm up her engine, then switched off again. She started as ever like a dream. Once I had a bit of trouble, but that was me, having knocked the choke lever on, thus trying to force rich fuel down her throat that she didn't want. You can't blame a girl for objecting to that. Another time the tall-guy Irish-Aussie surreptitiously messed with my cut-out switch, so I was left kicking the starter for a while, obviously with no result. I saw him grinning at me and guessed what he'd done. All a bit of fun, but it gave me grey hairs for a few minutes.

Burketown, the first stop, was only 93 kms from Gregory Downs. Almost 50 bikes hurtled into town and began devouring food and coffee, leaving the locals stunned and lacking provisions for at least two seasons. I love Australian coffee shops and always enjoyed our brief stops at them. It's very easy for a Pom to forget he isn't in his own country when everything on the menu is in English.

Then again when I'm in Oz or Kiwiland, I miss those strange distortions of the English language one gets on foreign menus. In Greece once I had 'scrawbled eggs' and in Thailand 'massed potatoes'. My all time favourite however, comes from Spain, where someone asked a friend for the English equivalent of *aguacate* (avacado), but what the friend heard was *abogado*. What appeared in print on the menu was a wonderful salad consisting of 'tomatoes, lettuce and lawyers', an *abogado* being a Spanish lawyer.

Burketown is on the Albert River and has a population of just under 200. (About the size of my Suffolk village, back in the old United Kingdom). Burke and Wills, the explorers, went past here on their way to the Gulf of Carpenteria. This is where I saw another of those wonderful Morning Glory clouds which can reach sometimes to a 1000 kms in length. Isn't that as long as Britain? It was great to ride under it, trying to get from one end to the other.

Local weather is back to front if you want ideal conditions: hot humid and wet summers, but warm dry winters. Cyclones are not unknown in the streets of Burketown.

The area is rich in fossils and this is one of the regions where the giant Doom Duck, which I mentioned earlier, roamed the landscape in prehistoric times.

Nowadays it's a large fish that draws the tourists. The barramundi or 'silver jack', a South East Asia game fish. It's at home in fresh or salt water. Its Australian name (I am told) means 'big scaly one' in the language of a tribe that lived near Rockhampton. These fellahs get to 1.5 metres in length. An interesting fact about this big fish is that if there's an imbalance in their numbers - say, 100 girl fish, to only 50 boy fish - 25 of the girl fish will change their sex to even up the numbers. Real gender benders. That's what I'm told. I believe it to be true.

The World Barramundi Fishing Championships are conducted out of Burketown. If you're a good angler you can win $2600 dollars for the heaviest single catch. Where I come from angling is the most popular sport, but you have to eat all you catch. I would rather catch a cod than a barramundi.

You can also find freshwater crocodiles in the region around Burketown. These prehistoric throwbacks aren't as hungry or ferocious as their salt water cousins up in the Gulf of Carpenteria and don't normally eat tourists. I imagine they still have a nasty bite, so be careful when petting them.

Back on the road again, grinding along. Some of the riders were fairly hefty blokes, quite wide in the beam. I often tucked myself behind one of these substantial characters and used them as a windbreak. What I could never understand was that if they wanted to go fast, they did, and I had a job catching them, even though I was half their size.

Next stop was the Leichhardt River, by way of Gunpowder Creek and Fiery Creek. The Leichhardt was named after Friedrich Wilhelm Ludwig Leichhardt, explorer and naturalist. His name sounds a little Germanic to me, but apparently he was a Russian. After several expeditions in the interior, Leichhardt vanished, as so many do in that wilderness even today. His body was never found but only in 2006 the remains of a shotgun bearing his name were discovered near Stuart Creek in Western Australia.

After navigating the historic Leichhardt River the postie caravan came to the worst track I have ever seen. It crossed the bush like a twisted red scar on the villainous face of the Outback. There was bull dust lurking in every crevice. On its surface were scattered loose gravel, rocks, sand and worst of all, corrugations. It had been gouged both ways, long and wide. There were horizontal ruts that resembled a corrugated iron and lateral ruts that grabbed the wheels and gripped them hard to prevent the rider from steering. In the first few kilometres many riders bit the dust. I was one of them.

I saw Ewan go over and give himself a very nasty crack in the ribs. Some people in a four-wheeler stopped to help him back on his feet. A few minutes later I hit thick bull dust on the edge of the track and went over the bars. On this occasion I wasn't going very fast and was more humbled than hurt.

I suppose the worst thing about that ride was having my bones shaken for nearly 200 kms. How the bikes stood the juddering of those corrugations were beyond me, because all I could hear was the rattling of metal on metal. How the tyres never burst was again a miracle. I know my body suffered from this hour on hour shaking. It nearly drove me crazy.

At one point I decided not to ride on the track but to go on the edge of the bush, which was a little flatter. Unfortunately every so often there was a natural ditch coming out of the bush which led right up to the edge of the dust road. I hit one of these side-on ditches at medium speed and once more flew through the air with the greatest of ease.

Unhurt again, I climbed back on the saddle and set off along the proper track, saying to hell with my internal organs if they wanted to change places I could do nothing about it. I had a headache from the constant rattling of my whole frame. I could see other riders having the same trouble, but the best of them seemed able to glide over the ruts. It was one of the worst few hours of my life. I thought it would never end.

When I had about 60 kms to reach Normanton and despair was at its peak, I decided to try to emulate the good riders. They were going at a much faster speed than me, so I assumed that speed was the answer, that one could skim over the ruts at a higher velocity. I picked up my speed, until I was going somewhere between 60 and 70.

Of course, the faster you go the less time you have to see danger on the track. I didn't see the huge lateral rut that trapped my front wheel until I was in it. The rut had a twist in it at the end which knocked aside my front wheel. This time I sailed through the air like a bird. I didn't land like one, though, I came down like a bread pudding. The track was iron hard. It knocked all the wind out of me and I gulped on red dust.

For a few minutes I just lay there in mild shock, looking up at the sky. I remember seeing little puffy clouds. I was hurting in several places, so I tested myself bit by bit to see if there were any broken bones. Arms, legs, neck, back. It seemed there were no serious breaks. I got myself up and then dragged my bike to the edge of the road. A single rider came along, a bloke named Gary, who I always called 'One-R' since my own name has two r's in it.

'Are you OK?' he asked. 'Any real damage?'

'No,' I gasped, still winded. 'Just shaken up I think.'

He helped me off with my jacket to make sure there were no bones poking through the skin. I had a healthy black bruise developing on my right arm and some lacerations. Gary put some iodine on the cuts then asked me again.

'Are you sure you're all right?'

'I'm fine. I'll wait for the repair truck. You go on. I'll be OK.'

He rode off, leaving me to inspect my bike. One of the mirrors had smashed, my speedo had bent over the front wheel and was pointing away from the rider and there were one or two other dints and scratches. Oh well, I thought, at least I'll get a ride now, from the repair truck. I won't have that last 60 kms to do over those sodding corrugations. It was my only consolation for the tumble and my aches and pains.

The truck arrived not long afterwards.

It was Dan himself. 'Had a fall?'

'Yep, I'm afraid I bent the bike a bit.'

'Let's have a look.'

I said, 'I must have been doing 70.'

Dan replied, 'The damage isn't that bad – your handlebars would have been bent.'

Most writers are prone to hyperboles. It's our stock in trade. We exaggerate. Why spoil a good story with the truth, is what we maintain. My dear wife is always straightening out the truth for me in front of people.

'There were at least a hundred of them,' I say, excitedly.

'Just twenty,' corrects my wife.

Wives do that to you. So do motorcycle challenge organisers. Dan was having none of it. So I guess I was probably doing less that 70, but how much less I don't know. All I maintain now is I *was* doing 70 at some time, but probably at the time of the crash my speed had fallen to less than that figure. My body felt it was 70, OK?

He took the broken mirror off, then straightened the speedo before testing it by spinning the wheel. Within a few minutes he had the bike in shape again. A horrible feeling was creeping over me. I really wanted that ride to Normanton, yet I knew I would be a failure if I took one. No chance of even having the choice though. Dan saw to that.

'Right, off you go,' he said, holding the bike so that I could climb back into the saddle. 'See you at Normanton.'

'Thanks Dan,' I said, choking back something that was stuck in my throat. 'Yeah, see you.'

Sore in a very many places, I started off again, my teeth rattling, my bones rattling, my liver changing places with my kidneys. It turned out it wasn't so bad. I only had 30 kms before the road conditions changed to a hard surface. I cruised into Normanton, missed the sign to the Rodeo grounds (where we were camping for the night) and had to ask two aboriginal young ladies for directions.

'What?' one of them asked.

They obviously didn't understand my English accent.

'The rodeo grounds?' I tried again, in an Aussie accent, which I'm pretty good at by the way.

They still looked at me as if I'd flown in from Mars.

I mimed an imitation of riding a bucking horse.

Still no comprehension in their eyes.

'Rodeo grounds. Rodeo,' I cried, desperately.

'Oh,' said the older girl, 'the *Rodeo Grounds*.'

To my way of thinking she hadn't said it any different to my mimicking of an Aussie accent.

They both pointed back the way I'd come.

'Thanks ladies.'

Once in the camp I was met by Pete.

'I hear you had a tumble.'

'Three,' I admitted, 'but only one really counted – the other two were just falling-over-sideways tumbles.'

'It happens,' he said. 'I had one last year.'

'Just one?'

'Hurry up and get your shower, we're going down to the Purple Pub,' he answered.

Sure enough, everyone gathered at the Purple Pub, a local tavern painted – you guessed it – purple.

It was a good evening. Good food, rugby on the television, several drinks to heal the pain in my limbs and body. Josie arrived in an ambulance with her foot in a plastic bag, but able to carry on the ride. Ewan told me how he went over his handlebars after hitting a large polythene water pipe. That must have been when I saw him take his tumble. 'Not necessarily,' he said, 'I took a bigger one later.' Others have parted company with their Hondas today. Victims of combination of corrugations, loose gravel and bull dust. I don't feel too bad, just a little upset with myself that I had actually contemplated a lift in the ute. I wanted to do all the stages with my bum on the saddle.

The best laugh I had that night was when John fell off his chair – I don't think he was even drunk at the time.

At one point in the day, I can't remember when, we had all crowded round an 8.64 metre salt water croc – not a real one, of course, but a statue – for a photo. Of course someone had to crawl into its mouth and have just his head and shoulders protruding. Anyway, this was a crocodile famous for its length, and why shouldn't it be? Over thirty feet of ravenous beast wouldn't be out of place on King Kong's island.

The meal at the Purple Pub was good, but halfway through I went to the bar to get a drink. One of our guys was telling the barman a long and windy joke. The barman was leaning on his bar with his eyes glazing over when I asked for a drink. He turned round to get me one and the guy telling the joke said, 'Hang on, I've got another one for you. There's this bloke . . .'

The barman whipped back round and said, 'Shit man, I nearly went to sleep during the last one.'

Nothing so blunt as an Aussie barman. The joke teller moved away, looking hurt, but at least I didn't have to wait to get my drink.

Later a local woman sidled up to Pete, saying, 'You married?' 'Yes I am,' Pete told her. 'Oh dear. Well never mind then, have you got a few cents you can spare?' Pete reached into his pocket and produced a coin. She took it and went straight to the bar and asked for a drink, whereupon the barman sighed deeply and told her, 'Look, Alice, you can't beg for money in here. You'll have to leave.' The woman made a face and went back to Pete and said, 'Come on, we've got to go to another pub, they won't serve us in this bloody place.' Pete of course stayed firmly in his seat, but we had a good laugh at her cheek.

DAY EIGHT

'Morning, Bill.'

'Morning!'

(This was Bill the American, a genial bloke from Arizona who worked in East Asia).

'Morning, Bill.'

'Morning!'

(This was Bill the Aussie, a writer of non-fiction histories. Very tall, very elegant for an Aussie.)

'Morning, Bill.'

'Morning!'

(This was . . .)

Heck, if you shouted 'Bill!' in the morning, about a dozen replies would come from all sides. Just like that oldie, if you yell Jock down the hatch of the engine room of a seagoing vessel (or rather more lately, a spacegoing starship) someone is bound to appear wiping his hands on an oily rag.

I stared out over the landscape. One of the two Cuzzies had accidentally hit a kangaroo over the last few days and unfortunately killed it stone dead. The rider and his bike were undamaged, so I understood. How this can happen with a Honda 110 is astonishing, kangaroos being big fellahs and bikes and blokes being a great deal smaller. Accidents like this were rare, but they did happen on occasion. A kangaroo had almost jumped on my bike earlier. It managed to swerve away when it was almost on me. Something spooks the creatures, out in the bush (maybe the bike engines?) and they just bounce off at high speed, crossing the highway if it's in their path.

There were also non-indigenous creatures out there. Wildcats, camels, wild pigs. I had been reading about the camels. Apparently when they were first introduced to Australia they came with Arab camel drivers. The writer of the article also said that when a camel driver died the lead camel was always killed and buried with him. Tradition.

I imagined a little scene in the Outback with the lead camel waking up and seeing the stiff body of his driver lying nearby, thinking, 'Oh crap!' and trying to make a run for it. This would account for all the wild camels now roaming the antipodean desert. Escapees from a sort of camel *suttee*. I didn't see any wild camels this trip but they had seen them last year. I think Pete took one or two photos of a herd.

I saw wild pigs, big ugly fellahs, but they were always on the side of the road, having been struck dead by traffic. These cadavers were usually bloated to twice their normal size and smelling fairly ripe. The stink would wrap around you like clingfilm as you rode past, reluctant to let you go. There was also a danger of hitting these carcasses and going over the bars, especially late in the day when the tiredness came on.

I was on the lookout for my first wild camel carcass.

After breakfast at the Purple Pub, we set out for Karumba, a small town on the Gulf of Carpenteria. So far the trip had been totally linear, but Karumba was a sort of side-shoot, a day trip to the seaside. Our eventual destination was Croyden – no, not one south of London – an old mining town on the way back to the east coast.

Karumba! Doesn't Bart Simpson say that, ever so often? *Aye, karumba*! I think I used to say it too, when I was a kid. Anyway, this offshoot was a pleasant diversion, across marshy country and close to mangrove swamps. The sky was full of those beautiful birds the brolgas, majestic as the herons of my own Suffolk waterlands. I did not tire of seeing flocks of them above me and more than once almost ended up in the ditch through not paying attention to where I was going.

Karumba is a fishing town. Prawns and barramundi apparently earn somebody in the region $130 million dollars a year. That's a lot of dosh. On approaching the town I saw a sign: WELCOME TO KARUMBA – POPULATION SMALL, BUT WE LOVE THEM ALL. Nice way to tell people to drive carefully. The Outback towns were fond of their signs. One of them, no doubt suffering a drought, said: WANNA BATH? - BYO WATER.

I would have liked to visit Sweers Island, 30-odd miles out from Karumba, but my little 21 was unfortunately not aquatic.

Sweers Island is home to about fifty species of bird. Charles Darwin dropped off there on his way around the world in the Beagle. He might have met the Kaiadilt people who it seems traditionally use the island for seafood gathering. That redoubtable sea captain Flinders gave the place a name in English, though undoubtedly it had one anyway in another language. He called it Sweers after a politician. Personally I wouldn't even name a dunny after a politician – or maybe I would – but only a dunny.

Captain Flinders and Captain Cook are well thought of in Oz, which is rare considering they're Poms. There's railway stations, streets, squares and even towns named after them. Good blokes, apparently, who navigated much of that which needed navigating back in the days when hardly anything had been mapped or charted. And so far as I know, neither of them were whingers, which goes down well with the local populace. Good on yer, captains courageous.

'You want to see the sea?' asked Pete, as we arrived in Karumba. 'There's quite a bit of it.'

So there was. A lot of sea. Blue too.

The first thing I saw above the beach was a sign which said, 'Watch out for salt water crocodiles.' It said it in English of course, but it also had a huge 'ACHTUNG!' and then said it more emphatically in German. Perhaps the crocs don't eat Frenchmen or Italians? Or maybe the Germans are particularly careless with their bodies? Who knows, I know I wasn't going to go swimming off that damn beach, which incidentally was being churned up by reckless young men on postie bikes when I arrived. They were having a sand party. I wasn't skilled enough to do the doughnuts and other stuff they were making their Hondas do, but it looked great fun.

Schoolteacher Josie's bike now had training wheels on the back. Someone had found the wheels in a garage sale and fitted them on for a joke. Richard-the-mechanic did not approve and they were removed a little later.

Pete and I went for a quiet coffee. I tried another of those double-shot long blacks that he always kicks his system off with. I was getting used to them. Whether I'd ever get to *like* them was another matter. They certainly got the blood racing round the arteries.

We were supposed to be visiting the barramundi factory and I had been looking forward to seeing a live one of these fish, but the factory was closed. Someone had forgotten it was Sunday. Apparently Aussies don't work on Sunday, which is pretty slack of them when you come to think about it. Still, we zoomed around town like the Wild Ones, and had a good look at everything before heading back towards Normanton.

John told us later that he had come across a broken down road train, a monster that had been stilled.

'The driver was kicking the wheels and calling it all sorts of ugly names,' John said. 'The vehicle was stuck halfway across the road and had seized on the turn. When I arrived they'd got two tow vehicles trying to shift it, but it didn't look as though it was going to move.'

Like trying to get a dead diplodocus out the way, I should imagine.

John didn't get any photos which was a shame.

The ride to Croyden was long and hazy. One of those stretches of bitumen which can make you sleepy. I hate that feeling when your eyes begin closing and you have to force them open with muscles you don't usually use. On those occasions I sang lustily to myself, old folk songs, old scout songs, anything, it didn't matter because it was all inside my helmet. No one else could hear and that was a blessing.

(I was once lost for 48 hours in the Yemen wilderness as a boy scout of 13 years – the maps were poor and a companion and I ended up circumnavigating an extinct volcano - and I sang the same songs then, only at that time brown kites, gazelles and pi-dogs were within earshot and I'm told they registered a complaint with the British Embassy.)

One way to make the journey on bitumen go faster was to lean forward and flatten yourself against the handlebars, thus presenting a low target for the wind. (Sit up and you act like a sail-brake). I used this method, as did others, for overtaking some of the larger members of the ride. And for going up long hills. I could get past Pete easily on a hill, though he still argues the fact. I passed QUASI-MOTO on this run, who took umbrage at my audacity and immediately repassed me. STEADY and EDDIE were there, and CUZZIE BRO 1 and CUZZIE BRO 2, the two cousins who rode together.

Still, the wide open spaces of Australia amazed me as I rode along. If I was to get poetic (which I sometimes do) I would say it filled my spirit with something quite extraordinary. I have never been to anywhere like it. The deserts of the Middle East come close – I got a similar feeling when standing on the pink sands of Wadi Rum in Jordan – but Australia is unique in its atmosphere. I would like to have captured the feeling of riding through the open countryside of Queensland, and bottled it. In my great old age I would open that bottle and take a draught 'Aussie Outback' for I'm sure it would be more invigorating than any drug or medicine.

Driving in Australia is in complete contrast to the other country where I spend a great deal of time: Spain. Andalucia has its wide open spaces of course, its mountain fastnesses and its red-and-yellow coloured landscape, but when I'm there I find myself driving mostly through *pueblos blancos*, the white villages in the hills, with their ever-narrowing streets.

I can't count the times I've driven into a town or village in Southern Spain on a normal width road, only to discover that within a few yards my wing mirrors are brushing the walls of houses on both sides of the car. I once mistakenly went down one of these funnels in a village in the Sierra Nevadas and realised we were not going to emerge out the other end of the street without ripping the doors off the hire car. I had to turn round. This involved asking a very obliging senora to open the front door of her home so that I could reverse over her stoop. She was very generous and helpful, and so were her neighbours, who all emerged from their houses to give me advice on inching the corner of my car into her living room. By the time I actually managed to turn the vehicle the sweat was pouring from my brow – most of it due to embarrassment and humiliation – while the villagers all cheered and clapped. There was probably more than a little sarcasm behind that applause.

Croyden was a welcome sight. We camped at the Rodeo Grounds again. The Shire Council were looking after us here in this old goldmining town. Would you believe there were once 5000 gold mines around this district? Once we'd tented up, seen to our bikes and showered, we got a talk from one of the local officials who shall remain unnamed.

'We used to have a shit-load of bawdy houses and pubs, and now we're down to one pub,' he said, 'but we're still on the map, with a shit-load of sheep, and a shit-load of cattle . . .' He was great. I wish he'd been my history teacher at school. I listened to his talk with undivided attention. He had one of those Outback accents which you only hear in old black-and-white movies about sheepshearers and flying doctors. He used a shit-load of phrases I'd never heard before in my life.

DAY NINE

The countryside changed today from flat bush with a scattering of dwarf trees to hilly rainforest and curving roads. There were pretty wattle trees by the roadside covered in yellow blossoms. We were heading for the Newcastle Range of hills, staying at a camp site with normal campers. It was not a long ride to Innot Springs, 386 kms, the majority of it on bitumen. An easy day then, for most of us. However, Murray - who usually rides with Cam and Scotty-the-clown - told the story of Cam's mishaps. It seemed Cam's bikes were triple cursed. He'd had two, which had busted, and was on his third, which still wasn't going well. The three of them stopped and Scotty checked the air filter and found '. . . enough dirt to fill a sandshoe'. After that Cam's machine went along fine until, '. . . he blew the front tyre.'

So not all bikes were dream machines like my 21.

Today's Running Sheet was very short. Only six entries from Croydon to Innot Springs village, going through Georgetown, Mount Surprise and Mount Garnet.

Out of Georgetown, Mount Garnet and Mount Surprise I was interested mainly in the last, which has a pub, two cafes and a petrol station. My sole interest being that I am a Yorkshireman and the town was founded by Ezra Firth, who was also from Yorkshire. All three towns have had minerals and metals in their veins, from gold, to copper, to tin. There's also a few gemstones around. Gem fossicking is one of the local sports and enjoyed by residents and tourists alike.

The ride itself, for me, was fairly uneventful. I can't remember much about it, except that we were travelling through different terrain and there was a good bit of wildlife about. When we arrived at Innot Springs we had a hot bath waiting. The camp site boasted natural hot-water baths which had their source in a spring that bubbled from the Nettle Creek. Pete and I plunged in, going from one bath to another, with rising heat, washing the dust of ages from our bones.

After dinner that night, I managed to phone Annette from a landline, and at last got through. We exchanged news. She had actually phoned Bev Kidby a couple of days earlier and been told I was fine. Annette had been having an exciting time in the Atherton Tablelands north of Innot Springs and wasn't that far away. She'd seen much more wildlife than me, including tree kangaroos, and of course the platypus, plus a whole variety of birds. Part of her time had been spent on a horse ranch with some Quakers who refused to take any money for her keep.

It was good to hear her voice again. I once spent a whole year at the beginning of our marriage without doing so, having been posted to Aden by the R.A.F. in a time when telephoning from such an outpost was hardly possible. An emergency would have done it, but we went the whole year without the world collapsing around us. It seems quite incredible now that in those days we were only able to correspond by letter. Those letters were treasured of course and now, with cellphones, such times seem to belong to ancient history.

'I've been leeched again,' she told me. 'Buggers!'

Annette is very attractive to leeches. They smell her from two miles away and head straight for her nice legs. Once in central Malaysia she had kindly fed a couple of leeches for an hour. Afterwards we couldn't stop the bleeding, leeches having pumped her full of anti-coagulant. In the end she was slopping along with a shoe full of blood. We were due to fly home that day and she had to throw her trainers, socks and all, into a waste bin before boarding the aircraft barefoot. When we finally got home, almost a day later, she couldn't wash the dried blood off her feet because our septic tank had backed up and the shower room was full of sewage. Happy days.

On my way back to my tent I heard something ominous. Four or five of the riders were outside their tents vomiting. I've had food poisoning once or twice before in my life and I knew the sound. Poor buggers, I thought, they've either drunk some bad water, or eaten some bad food, and now they're feeling bad. I went to bed, the sound of rainbow yawns still disturbing the quiet of the evening.

An hour in bed and I was up again and, like a few others, was running for the toilets. I must have gone about a twenty times that night. Each time I got back into bed the churning in my stomach started and I would be up again and visiting the dunny. I took two imodium tablets and some salt water. At six-thirty, having had no sleep and with bowels that were spurting nothing but dirty water I went to see Dan.

'I don't think I can ride today,' I said, miserably.

Dan rolled his eyes and sighed. 'I'll need to hire a coach,' he said.

'Is it that bad? That many?'

'Well,' and he stared me directly in the eyes, 'up until now no one has actually said they're *not* riding, except you.'

I got the look and I got the drift.

Get on your bike, you whinging Pom.

I walked away and for the first time began to throw up. I must have got rid of the lining of my stomach in that bout, but afterwards I felt a little better. I got some more rehydration salts, drank about a gallon of water, and took a handful of imodium pills. I stayed away from breakfast and stood there by my bike feeling exhausted and frail. The imodium worked now that I'd taken a healthy dose. Nevertheless I chucked a couple of toilet rolls into the milk crate on the back of the bike. When the call came I got on my machine and set off. I planned to stop every 50 kms to drink a half-litre of water.

DAY TEN

My plan worked quite well. We were travelling due east from Innot Springs to Cooktown. There was some dirt road, but not a great deal. I was getting used to dust and grit under my wheels. But it was a long hot day ahead. 377 kms, passing through Atherton and Mareeba. Refuel stop today was at Mount Carbine roadhouse. I stayed by myself, sometimes with no other rider in sight, and just banged along the highway thinking about the end of the day. The scenery was quite pretty, with hills to look at and trees in partial bloom. It would have been a pleasant ride, if I wasn't feeling so sick. However, I was grateful to Dan for getting me back on the bike. I know I would have felt cheated at the end of the ride if I'd missed even one single stage.

Atherton itself was a small pleasant town. Where it was, was more important than what it was. It was the gateway to the Atherton Tablelands, where Annette was staying. The Tablelands is a high cool plateau, rich with wildlife and scenery. There were scores of different birds there, from the Cassowary to the Double-eyed Fig Parrot to the Papuan Frogmouth. Among its animals were dingos, bandicoots and echidnas (those giant hedgehogs of the bush). It also boasted, amongst its reptiles, the second most venomous snake in the world, the Eastern Brown Snake. I thought its name was pretty tame for a such a poisonous fellah. It surely should be called something like, the Deadly Silver Medalist, or the Instant Killer Runner-up.

An Eastern Brown Snake was seen slithering onto a gas station forecourt during the ride.

Not only were there live wonders on the Atherton Tablelands, but natural wonders too, with over 13 waterfalls, including the Dinner Falls and the Zillie Falls. I wondered how many of these beasts and sights Annette had seen, as I rattled through Atherton on my trusty machine, little knowing that she was there on a bus watching me, and a few dozen other pretend posties, beating up the tarmac. She couldn't recognise me of course, because we all looked more or less alike in our riding gear and on identical bikes. Nevertheless, the whole bus knew about her husband and kept pointing riders out as they shot past, saying, 'Is that him?'

I trundled out into the bush again, still feeling very weak and wobbly, and managed to shoot past the refuel truck and about thirty bikes and riders, not wanting company at that moment. Luckily I stopped myself just a few hundred yards along the road. One of the trucks came out with Richard the mechanic driving.

'What's up, mate?' he asked me, climbing out of the cab. 'That's the refuel stop back there.'

'Oh,' I said, desultorily. 'Sorry - missed it.'

'Well, get your backside on your bike and find it again, eh?'

I did as I was told and when I got there Richard had a can of gas ready to put in my machine.

'Go and sit in the shade,' he said, kindly. 'I can see you're still feeling crook.'

He filled my tank and put a full five-litre spare in my milk crate. Good old Richard. He was now due to go in my last will and testament, if I ever saw dear old merry England again.

Pete came to then. 'I saw you shoot past - still chucking up?'

'Not so much, but I feel like I've been in a washing machine on full cycle for four hours.'

'Ah, you'll be fine,' he said.

The afternoon was incredibly hot. I still stopped every 50 kms and met a wizened Grey Nomad on one of my stops. He was as dried up as an ancient gum tree by the wind and the sun. He had no teeth, but he could talk for both Ireland and Australia. He told me all about the 'Beezer' bike he'd owned when he was a young man - back in Captain Cook's time I guessed by the look of him. I sat there about an hour listening to him. He had the gift all right. Although I hardly understood a word he was saying - it was all biker and bush talk - I found him a really interesting character and would like to have had a pint with him.

'Tell you what, mate, I miss that Beezer more than I miss a darling wife,' he told me, chuckling. 'Bloody hell, she was a goer that bike was. Give few bucks now to get her back.' And his eyes went all misty as his thoughts disappeared somewhere back in the distant past.

I looked nervously at his RV but no irate lady appeared at the window. I guessed he was on his own, but whether his spouse had passed on, or he was divorced, or indeed he may have been single all his life, I did not know. I left him by the roadside and he promised to look us postie bike challengers up when he got to Cooktown.

I never saw him again.

I did look up 'Beezer' on the internet later: the bike he was referring to was the 650cc BSA Thunderbolt of the 1960s.

At the end of the day I was feeling a lot better. My innards were stable, but as always with the tail end of the ride, I was getting very very tired. Eight hours on a blistering highway, following a white line, is sure to make the eyes want to close. I had to fight to keep them open. I've always been a power nap man. When I write for hours at a stretch there's always a point where I can't keep my eyes open any longer and I simply get off my chair, lay on the floor, and nap for twenty minutes. After which I'm as refreshed as fizzy drink. You can't do that while you're riding a bike, so as usual I ended up singing loudly to myself inside my helmet, which is a bit like a bathroom opera. Of course, *desperately* tired and you have to pull over and throw water in your face, but when you're very close to the destination this is a hard thing to do.

I was getting passed by other riders - NZ MALE SERVICE - went shooting past me, showing me his back. But by that time we were sweeping the bends of the hills leading down to Cooktown, which was a great pleasure. The town is of course named after Captain Cook, who is greatly revered on the east coast of Australia, at least by non-aboriginals. (I confess I have no idea what the Aboriginal people think of him.) Cook was the first European in this region, and afterwards came the redoubtable Captain Flinders. Both mapped the area, including the Great Barrier Reef, and their statues and names are found in several Australian cities and towns. Cook's Cottage, the home of his parents, was dismantled in 1934 and reassembled stone by stone in Melbourne, Victoria.

James Cook was a Scot with a mother who had the unlikely name of Grace Pace. (What were her parents thinking of?) Happily she later became Grace Cook when she married James' father.

Captain Cook is of course one of Britain's most distinguished explorers. He made three Pacific voyages and mapped the coastline of New Zealand. He named many places on his journeys throughout the world, including Botany Bay, but my favourite is a small town in Queensland which he called '1770'. I met someone from 1770 when on a trip to Karunda. He seemed quite pleased that Cook had run out of names and had fallen back on the year of discovery.

Cooktown is beautiful. Overlooked by Grassy Hill, which sounds as green as it looks, there are gardens and parks blooming everywhere. We set up our tents in a camping park under the shade of a grove of eucalyptus trees. It was paradise after the dust and grit of the Outback. I had a hammering head but a couple of pain killers took care of that. I also started to feel hungry again. The riders were all cheerful, smiling at each other, talking about cool beer. Not that there had been any animosity on the ride that I'd noticed. A couple of irritating moments, but nothing to start a war about. But Cooktown was such a blissful place you couldn't help but feel like singing and dancing.

I did inspect the gum trees closely. On an earlier trip to Oz I learned of two types of eucalyptus tree: black box and river red. One type, and I couldn't remember which, was called the 'widow maker' because huge branches snapped off without warning and dropped on unwary people below. Which was it? I kept asking myself, nervously, as there was no space to camp which was not below the heavy-looking spreading arms of these beautiful but deadly gum trees.

It was in that Cooktown camping park that I saw my first 'swag' - a great Australian invention. A swag is a not much more than a sleeping bag with a cover, but ideal if you want to see the stars as you drop off to sleep. I was determined to get one at some time. You need good weather before you decide to use one of course, but heck, who knows that I won't be visiting Oz again in the near future. I'm only 68.

Once again, the meal that evening was superb, being provided by the local Little Athletics Club. And as usual, we gave the ladies who cooked it a great round of applause for their brilliant efforts. The whole trip had been like that. I had come on the ride thinking I would shed some pounds, but if anything I put them on. I went to bed as usual, around 8 pm, along with most others. I don't think anyone stayed awake beyond nine. It had been a long and tiring day. It had been a long and tiring 10 days. One more day and we were back in real life again.

At least I wasn't chucking out from both ends.

THE LAST DAY

This was the day we had all been looking forward to. Not simply because it was the last day, but because we were going on the Bloomfield Track through the Daintree Rainforest. All being well we would be in Cairns for the mid to late afternoon. The end of the ride. There we would hand over our darling machines to the Rotary Club, who were going to sell them and donate the money to various charities. It would be like parting from a courtesan. One or two riders were going to buy their bikes for the second time, and keep them. For Poms like me, this was impractical. We'd have to ship them back to the UK at great expense and I'd already spent a great deal on this expedition. With fares, the cost of the challenge, and various other expenses, it had come to around £5000. I'd been saving that for my next car, but what the heck, you can't put a price on the great Outback experience we'd had.

Daintree rainforest is over 135 million years old. The oldest rainforest on Earth. Nearly 500 feathered friends live there, including a dozen species that are found nowhere else in the world. It has the most diverse range of plants and animals on the planet. It's 1200 square kilometres of frogs, marsupials, butterflies and birds. On the human front the Kuku Yalariji people inhabited and lived off the forest for over 9000 years. The non-aboriginals, who followed in Captain Cook's footsteps, began logging the area, but were later halted by the Australian Federal Government who made it a World Heritage area.

'There's a steep hill on the track,' Pete warned me, 'after a sharp bend. You'll need to be in first gear. If you don't start it in first, you won't make it to the top and it's a hell of a job trying to kick-start on a forty-five degree slope.'

'You slide back down?'

'If the dirt's loose enough, yes.'

The moment we entered the Daintree, I knew this was Nirvana. I love trees, wildlife and flora. This place had the lot.

I had to be on the watch for giant tree frogs (14 cms long!), man-eating crocodiles, golden orb spiders and musky rat-kangaroos. Daintree was also home to that most famous of live bush-tucker meals, the witchetty grub, a fellah I would just as soon not meet if it's all the same to you.

There were some beautiful trees, of course, as magnificent as cathedrals, others with pretty foliage and blossoms to gladden the heart. But there were also a few bad guy plants. We had to watch out for the Stinging Tree, which brings you up in large blisters that are extremely painful. Next to him in the gang was the Wait-a-while Vine, which apparently rips you to bits with its small spikes. Then there's the Idiot Fruit, which you mustn't get mixed up with the Wild Ginger that also grows here. Idiot Fruit will kill you stone dead with its heavy dose of strychnine. Annette loves ginger and I just hoped she hadn't gone wandering in the forest and seen something that looked tasty.

The Bloomfield track itself was bumpy dirt and rocks, quite wide in most places, but with not just one steep hill (as my Aussie chum had implied) but dozens of them. We went up and down a hundred times, my heart stopping on the downstrokes as I hurtled towards a narrow v-shaped dip below before the next steep climb. The Big One that Pete had mentioned was attacked by a huge crowd of us at once. I almost made it to the top (in first gear naturally) when someone slewed sideways right in front of me. I had to brake sharply, which brought me to an immediate stop on a hill which flies had trouble clinging to. Somehow, I managed to struggle up the last few metres, but it wasn't fun while all around was the chaos of loud machines battling with the landscape.

The next obstacle was the river at the Wujal Wujal Aboriginal Community. We had three rivers to cross, or possibly the same river three times, with the water up to our wheel hubs. This was salt water crocodile country, so eyes were skinned.

In the last few days a Belgium tourist in the region had caused his arm to be chewed by a salt-water croc when he stupidly splashed water on the croc's face 'because it wasn't moving'. It could move pretty quickly, actually, and clamped its massive jaws on his forearm. He got more than the photograph he was after: teeth marks all along his flesh. He'd actually been extremely lucky to escape. Most crocs of this huge variety spin over and over once they've got a grip on their victim, and the arms are twisted from their sockets. Either that or the victim is dragged down into the water and becomes a feast for the beast. Crocs often stash the remains under submerged logs to allow them to rot. Seemingly humans taste better when the meat tenderises and falls off the bone.

An Aussie croc has been known to take a victim in three inches of water, so the shallowness of our river, about two feet, was no protection.

The first crossing was easy, a shallow ford with a concrete base. The only hazard there were the 4x4 vehicles that wanted to go faster than we could. The next crossing was a wide creek with rushing, tumbling water and boulders and smooth stones for its bottom. Riders went over in swathes and singles, and were thrown this way and that by the uneven surface below, as well as having to contend with cold water over the tops of their boots. One or two machines bounced wrongly, cut out halfway over and had to be man-handled to the far shore.

I went across with John, whose bike conked out halfway over. I had a 4-wheel vehicle right on my tail so I had to bump my way awkwardly past him. Everyone was yelling at me and pointing to the car behind me, but I knew the blighter was there. I got a bit hot under the collar with all the shouting and started shouting back. No one could hear me cursing them of course, because my voice simply reverberated around my helmet and only served to deafen me. It was very frustrating and I rode off in a bit of a temper. There's nothing like a bit of a temper to help increase the usual velocity and the next thing I did was go down one of the hills at much too fast a pace, only to meet a truck coming round the bend at the bottom. It was taking up most of the track width.

Here's where my inexperience was my downfall, literally. Instinctively I reached for the rear brake on the right hand side of the handlebars. It wasn't there of course, because I wasn't riding the automatic I rode in England, but a Honda 110 which has a footbrake. The bike fishtailed and threw me off. I slammed jaw-first into a boulder on the edge of the track. The same arm that I'd hurt in the last tumble came between me and a hard place. I ended up in the dirt in a humiliating bundle of arms and legs and a twisted body.

'Are you all right? Can I help?'

It was the driver of the vehicle, looming over me.

I climbed awkwardly to my feet. I was embarrassed, as one is when one feels stupid. I wanted to get rid of him as soon as possible.

'Yes, I'm fine. Just a spill.'

'Sure?'

'Absolutely.'

'Anyone with you?'

'My support truck will be along in a minute.'

He stared at me for a while, then went to his own truck.

I gathered myself together, brushed the dust away as best I could, though me and the bike were covered. Inspecting 21 I noticed the gear lever was bent and the handlebars were twisted. I was straightening the bars when Andy arrived in the support truck.

'Come off?'

'Again,' I replied.

He sorted out the bike's bars but told me not to try and straighten the gear lever.

'It might snap off. You can still use it, can't you?'

I tried and found I could.

He looked into my eyes. 'Are you hurt?'

'Not seriously. There's a big lump on my arm and my jawbone's a bit out of kilter, but luckily my motocross helmet stopped me from breaking anything.'

It was fortunate. If I was wearing the half-face helmet I also owned, I would have had a broken jaw for certain. Thank you, Pete, for insisting that I buy the motocross helmet. I had quibbled at the expense of the thing, but it had saved me months of having my face wired up, and having to suck soft food through a tube, not to mention all the associated pain that goes with resetting broken mandibles.

'All right. On the bike.'

I got back on and a few minutes later crossed the river again. It was just as difficult at the last crossing, but this time I did it perfectly. Of course there were no witnesses present. Ain't that just the way of things? The longest putt of your life at golf is when you're a single, solitary player going round alone. The loveliest girl you pull is when you're on holiday without your mates. The biggest fish you catch is when all the other anglers have packed up and gone home.

Did you see that?

No, they didn't. Nobody saw it, because no one was there watching. And you can't tell them later, because they refuse to believe you, no matter how much sincerity goes into your tone.

I was now switchbacking the hills towards Cape Tribulation, where Captain Cook's ship came to grief. On my shoulder was a damn white truck that began to first annoy me, then anger me. Finally I stopped the bike and shouted at the driver.

'Why the hell don't you pass me?'

Andy poked his head out the side window and grinned.

'Sweeper truck, mate. You're the last rider.'

The last rider.

I had never been the last rider. I couldn't possibly be the *last* rider. I'd promised myself that wouldn't happen. Even just on a single short stage. It wouldn't matter a great deal to an experienced rider, but I was a beginner and it was really important for me not to look like one.

'There's one bloke back there,' I said, recalling passing a bearded rider savagely kicking the tyre of a prone machine way back on the trail. He had never passed me. 'Someone's behind me.'

'His bike broke down,' replied Andy. 'They took him and his machine in the repair truck.'

Shit! I was the last rider.

When I got to Cape Tribulation, the rest of them were just preparing to leave to catch the ferry across a much wider stretch of river. I had just enough time to grab a coke and get Lang to straighten my handlebars properly. Then I was back on the road again, but smooth bitumen this time. I ached a bit, but not enough to spoil the last day of the ride. Now the tarmac hummed under my tyres and there were enough bends in the road to make it an interesting ride. There was more traffic of course, but it was easy enough to let them pass, and usually they gave a friendly wave, which was pleasant.

A beautiful foot-long lizard crossed my path, running on high legs to keep its belly clear of the hot tarmac on the road. It made me think about the rainforest. I hadn't noticed a single bird or animal while I was in there. One of the most populated rainforest parks in the world and I had simply rattled through it on 21 without seeing a thing. That was upsetting. I made up my mind that I would come back again, on foot, and look for those creatures and plants that I'd missed this time round.

Finally we were on the Captain Cook Highway, the coastal road from Daintree to Cairns, which was a very pleasant twisty piece of bitumen with lots of sweeping up and down curves: a perfect end to a journey full of grit, dust and surprises. We gathered in a side road just inside the city, to slap each other's backs.

'We made it,' said John. 'Well done, Gazzer. Well done, Pete.'

John looked quite chuffed and I was feeling pretty good too. It could so easily have ended in disaster. One guy did not make it past the first day and that could so easily have been John or me.

It was of course Peter's second time around.

Pete nodded, saying, 'I set out with two priorities this year. Firstly, to stay on my bike, something I failed to do last year. Secondly, to make sure two you didn't kill yourselves.'

He had succeeded in both, firstly by using his previous year's expertise to stay glued to the Honda's saddle, secondly by passing on lots of good savvy to the green pommies. 'When you hit bull dust, drop down a gear and power through it . . .' Stuff like that which I had only listened to with half an ear, but which, when the bike started to fishtail and my heart rate went shooting off the scale, came back to me vividly. He had done a good job on both counts. There weren't many who hadn't come off their bikes and tasted the fine Australian dust.

When we were all in, Dan organised us into a long line. Then we cruised neatly in pairs into the heart of Cairns as if we were a police parade. Sadly though, only forty-six out of the original fifty. We entered and clustered together in a small park below the hotel where most of us were staying. Local press and well-wishers were there to welcome us back into the real world. After the pictures and the interviews, the Cairns' Rotary Club led us once again through the streets to a warehouse where they wrested our bikes from our firm grips. 21 was going to a new home. I hoped they'd appreciate her. She was a beaut.

The residue aches and pains of the ride would be with me for a while. My fingers would still be in a claw-like grip for many days afterwards. I had lumps and bruises on my arms and legs from fighting with boulders and dirt roads. Whenever I went to sleep I could see a white line stretching into infinity in my head. My backside would take a while to get any real feeling back into the buttocks.

The showers in the hotel ran red that afternoon, as riders washed every corner of their bodies, getting rid of the Outback dust. My riding clothes were put into plastic bags which Annette had brought with her. They carried half a continent in their seams. The white rim of my helmet was no longer white and never would be again. My boots, God bless them, could have belonged to one of Wellington's soldiers. They were shapeless lumps of leather ingrained with Australia. I would be going home carrying much of the Outback with me in my suitcase.

That evening we had a dinner to which the riders, organisers and Rotary people were invited. There we were presented with some treasured certificates and received a talk from a Rotarian. We learned where the money from the sale of the bikes was eventually going in the countries that needed it most:

+ 30,000 polio vaccinations

+ 200 cleft palate operations

+ 100 wheel chairs

As a side issue there was fund-raising for 11 community groups who assisted us with meals and bedspaces on our journey.

Good on yer, postie bike!

The following morning we shook hands with those who were up and about. Pete, John and I, and our wives, were going to Port Douglas to spend a week in a house with a swimming pool. Others were going home to tell their stories to their families, to their mates in pubs, and perhaps even stopping people on the street and regaling them with adventures tales. There had been a touch of the Ancient Mariner about this ride. It had been an extraordinary voyage through an immense mysterious land with hazy edges and shimmering shapes. A forever place where the sky is a huge dome of blue peppered with bits of white. A timeless dreamscape. Had it been 11 days and 4000 kilometres? It was an experience none the riders would ever forget, I'm sure. Friendships had been forged along with the memories.

Made in the USA
Charleston, SC
23 May 2014